M000019150

The God of Possible

Scripture quotations marked KJV are taken from the King James Version of the Bible.

Scripture quotations marked NKJV are taken from the New King James Version®. Copyright © 1982 by Thomas Nelson, Inc. Used by permission. All rights reserved.

Scripture quotations marked NIV are taken from the HOLY BIBLE, NEW INTERNATIONAL VERSION®. NIV®. Copyright © 1973, 1978, 1984, 2011 by Biblica, Inc.™ Used by permission. All rights reserved worldwide.

Scripture quotations marked NLV are taken from the New Life Version copyright © 1969 and 2003 by Barbour Publishing, Inc. Uhrichsville, Ohio 44683. All rights reserved.

Scripture quotations marked NLT are taken from the *Holy Bible.* New Living Translation copyright© 1996, 2004, 2015 by Tyndale House Foundation. Used by permission of Tyndale House Publishers, Inc. Carol Stream, Illinois 60188. All rights reserved.

Scripture quotations marked NASB are taken from the New American Standard Bible, © 1960, 1962, 1963, 1968, 1971, 1972, 1973, 1975, 1977, 1995 by The Lockman Foundation. Used by permission.

Scripture quotations marked HCSB are taken from the Holman Christian Standard Bible ® Copyright © 1999, 2000, 2002, 2003, 2009 by Holman Bible Publishers. Used with permission by Holman Bible Publishers, Nashville, Tennessee. All rights reserved.

Scripture quotations marked TLB are taken from The Living Bible © 1971 by Tyndale House Foundation. Used by permission of Tyndale House Publishers, Inc., Carol Stream, Illinois 60188. All rights reserved.

Scripture quotations marked ESV are from The Holy Bible, English Standard Version®, copyright © 2001 by Crossway Bibles, a publishing ministry of Good News Publishers. Used by permission. All rights reserved.

Cover Design: Greg Jackson, Thinkpen Design

Published by Barbour Books, an imprint of Barbour Publishing, Inc., 1810 Barbour Drive, Uhrichsville, Ohio 44683, www.barbourbooks.com.

Our mission is to inspire the world with the life-changing message of the Bible.

Member of the
Evangelical Christian
Publishers Association

Printed in China.

The God of Possible

DEVOTIONS & PRAYERS
FOR LIFE'S TRYING TIMES

Janet Ramsdell Rockey

BARBOUR BOOKS
An Imprint of Barbour Publishing, Inc.

Introduction

"But with God all things are possible."
MATTHEW 19:26 NASB

Why does God allow trials, even a season of trials, to affect our lives? Perhaps to build our trust that what we cannot see in our future, He can, and He will take us through. Because His Word is a lamp to our feet and a light on our paths, He illuminates one step at a time, allowing us to see either the benefits or hardships at different times.

Our heavenly Father controls all things. He commands every part of the massive universe. Planets orbit according to His will. Galaxies rotate within His harmony. Yet on earth, He cares about even a tiny sparrow's fall. Knowing almighty God personally through our relationship with the Lord Jesus Christ gives us an advantage in facing challenges. He loves us with an everlasting love, even when we doubt Him. Although we can't comprehend His ways, we can look back and see His presence woven through the tapestry of our circumstances.

Whether an incident brings reward or discipline, He always holds us in His loving arms. Beaten down and weary, we can trust God with every facet of every day because "with people this is impossible, but with God all things are possible" (Matthew 19:26 NASB).

The Ultimate Sacrifice

*And the L<small>ORD</small> God made clothing from
animal skins for Adam and his wife.*
G<small>ENESIS</small> 3:21 NLT

Adam and his wife took pleasure in an intimate relationship with God until they disobeyed Him. Instead of looking forward to their walk in the garden with Him, they hid in fear—a new discomfiting emotion that replaced their joy.

In her naivete, Eve succumbed to Satan's deception, and then she questioned God's goodness. Adam knew better but followed her example and ate. In wanton disobedience, they acted on Satan's lie rather than relying on God's truth, replaced God's will with their own, and doomed the human race and the world to the loathsome penalty of their sin.

God instituted the first sin offering to restore their fellowship with Him. An animal had to be slaughtered, the first shedding of blood, to make garments to cover their nakedness.

Humankind has wearied the Lord with our inherited rebellious nature ever since. But He planned a solution in eternity past. God provided the ultimate sacrifice, His own Son, not merely to cover our sin but to remove it as far from Him as the east is from the west.

*Gracious Father, we regret the times we weary You
with our own insolent stubbornness. Thank You for
Your long-suffering patience and love for us.*

Alignment with God

The LORD said to Samuel, "Listen to the voice of the people in regard to all that they say to you, for they have not rejected you, but they have rejected Me from being king over them."

1 SAMUEL 8:7 NASB

The Israelite elders clamored from selfish motives for Samuel to appoint a king for them. They wanted to imitate the surrounding pagan nations, effectively rejecting God as their true King. They failed to realize that conforming to pagan customs would weaken their spiritual connection to the Lord.

God instructed Samuel to anoint Saul as a prince, not a king, in order to deliver the people from the Philistines.

Saul reluctantly began his reign as a humble servant, with Samuel as his mentor. As his military success increased, so did his self-will and disobedience. He began to reshape the terms of worship, which led him to a disastrous end.

How often does this happen to us? In our rush to climb the career ladder, close the next deal, or gain secular recognition, do we forget to follow God's guidance? Then do we wonder why He disciplines us? Daily time in prayer and Bible reading enables us to remain in alignment with the Lord.

O God, our King, help us acknowledge Your sovereignty. Let all that we do bring honor and glory to You.

Nothing Too Difficult

"Behold, I am the LORD, the God of all flesh;
is anything too difficult for Me?"
JEREMIAH 32:27 NASB

Under King Zedekiah, the Israelites turned away from almighty God and offered incense to Baal, poured out drink offerings to other gods, and committed the most detestable abomination of all—sacrificing their babies to the fire of Molech. While false prophets told the king only what he wanted to hear, Jeremiah truthfully prophesied about the coming judgment on Jerusalem.

Because Judah sank into pagan idolatry, God judged the nation and allowed the king of Babylon to crush Jerusalem "by sword, by famine and by pestilence" (Jeremiah 32:36 NASB). The Chaldeans burned the city to the ground and took the survivors into captivity. As dismal as the situation looked, God used those wicked acts to bring about His plan.

In His mercy and at His appointed time, He gathered His people from distant kingdoms and returned them to their land. He restored them, and they worshipped Him. Just as He brought great calamity upon them, He also bestowed all the goodness He had promised them.

Do we weary God with our modern idolatries? If we turn back to Him, He will restore our fellowship with Him, for nothing is too difficult for God.

Lord God, thank You for Your
immeasurable mercy and love.

Higher Purpose

"But as for you, you meant evil against me;
but God meant it for good, in order to bring it
about as it is this day, to save many people alive."
GENESIS 50:20 NKJV

Joseph suffered hardships at the hands of his envious, hate-filled brothers. They mocked him, plotted his murder, and sold him to a caravan traveling to Egypt. There, he was sold again, faced sexual harassment and false accusations, and landed in jail.

Joseph probably wondered where the Lord was. According to the scriptures, God was with him all the time. Then Joseph rose to power, second only to Pharaoh.

When his brothers came to Egypt fifteen years later, fear and guilt gripped them when they realized he held authority over them. But Joseph understood that God's purpose was higher than acts of retaliation against his brothers. The tiny nation of Israel needed an incubation period to grow in number and strength, and God used Joseph to bring that about.

Many of us can relate to Joseph when a family member, friend, or colleague plots against us. While the other person meant it for evil, God meant it for good to give us an opportunity to glorify Him.

Gracious God, give us the faith of noble Joseph,
who remained devoted to You and sought Your
will in the midst of turmoil and strife.

Path of Blessing

*This is the plan determined for the whole world; this is
the hand stretched out over all nations. For the L*ORD
*Almighty has purposed, and who can thwart him?
His hand is stretched out, and who can turn it back?*
ISAIAH 14:26–27 NIV

Through the prophet Isaiah, God predicted the destruction of Assyria. Twenty years later, He fulfilled the prophecy when the angel of the Lord struck down 185,000 Assyrians in their camp.

He also predicted that Babylon, the jewel of kingdoms, the pride and glory of the Babylonians, would be destroyed. No human being would ever again inhabit that glorious city. To this day, it is nothing but ruins. Only wild animals live where magnificent buildings once stood.

Sometimes we feel like the ruins of Assyria or Babylon, devastated by our circumstances. But we will never suffer the fate of those pagan kingdoms that denied God. Throughout the Old Testament, we find messianic prophecies. The Messiah would be born of a virgin in Bethlehem, of the ancestry of Judah. He would be crucified, rise again, and ascend to the Father. In His sovereignty, God has provided a path of blessings for us through the fulfillment of the prophecy about His Son, Jesus Christ.

*Father, in our most devastating circumstances,
we seek Your path of blessings to comfort us.*

Unmerited Grace

*Then Job answered the Lord and said, "I know
that You can do all things, and that no
purpose of Yours can be thwarted."*

JOB 42:1–2 NASB

After a season of suffering and unjust criticism, Job listened in awe as God revealed His wisdom and power. The Lord rules over all His creation, yet He cares about each person.

When it was his turn to speak, Job humbly addressed the Lord, repenting in dust and ashes. He sought and found joy in sharing God's fellowship. At the end of his faith challenge, Job learned that he had no right to express his human disapproval of God's divine ways.

By restoring all that Job had lost and giving him even more, the Lord vindicated Job's faithfulness against Satan's initial challenge.

It is truly difficult not to complain when the Lord allows us to be subjected to tragedies or hardships. But by trusting His ultimate control, we learn to lean on His everlasting arms. When we feel like we can't take another step, He will carry us and sustain us. God is always with us.

Unwarranted calamity reveals God's mercy to us, His unmerited grace.

*Almighty and powerful God, we trust in
You to bring us through our difficult times.
Wrap us in Your loving arms.*

Limitless Possibilities

For no man of his seed shall prosper, sitting upon the throne of David, and ruling any more in Judah.

JEREMIAH 22:30 KJV

God cursed King Jeconiah (also known as Jehoiachin or Coniah) because of his wickedness. The Chaldeans took him to Babylon, where he spent the rest of his life in captivity. None of his descendants reigned after him.

God used this particular curse to exhibit His sovereignty in at least two ways.

Matthew's genealogy traces the royal line of Joseph through Solomon to Jeconiah. If not for Jeconiah's curse, Joseph might have been king instead of Herod at the time of Christ's birth. But God had a nobler plan for Joseph: to be the stepfather of the Messiah. Joseph heeded the instructions of God's messenger and took Mary as his bride, escorted her to Bethlehem, then fled to Egypt to protect them from Herod's murderous plot.

Luke's genealogy traces the true lineage of Jesus through Mary to Nathan, Solomon's brother. If Jesus had been born in the line of Joseph, the curse would have disqualified Him from sitting on the throne of David in the millennium. But God assured the Lord's future reign through Mary, since her ancestry didn't include Jeconiah.

Heavenly Father, open our eyes to Your sovereignty and let us witness Your limitless possibilities.

A Bountiful End

*Then the angel of the Lord appeared to the woman
and said to her, "Behold now, you are barren
and have borne no children, but you shall
conceive and give birth to a son."*

JUDGES 13:3 NASB

After many barren years, God blessed Manoah and his
wife with a son named Samson. When the angel of the
Lord announced the coming birth, Manoah prayed for
guidance to raise this special child. He learned his son
was designated to live an abstemious life as a Nazirite.

Samson violated his Nazirite status on numerous
occasions, yet God still used him to destroy the Philistines. Because he epitomizes a believer who fails but is
still used by God, we know that God can use stumbling
Christians for His glory. Chapter 11 in Hebrews even
lists Samson among the heroes of faith!

When our productivity slows to a stop, we often
feel barren. Maybe our business loses money or health
problems reduce our usefulness. The Lord can provide
a bountiful end to our desolate season, even if the
remedy seems chaotic or exasperating. God, in His
sovereignty, will use it to bring about His purpose for
our lives. Step back and watch Him move.

*Father God, let us remember Your sovereignty to work
Your glory through any situation and anyone.*

Godly Wisdom

"If you do this thing and God so commands you, then you will be able to endure, and all these people also will go to their place in peace." So Moses listened to his father-in-law and did all that he had said.
EXODUS 18:23–24 NASB

Moses acted as the judge and mediator for the Israelites in the wilderness. From dawn to dusk, they inundated him with their disputes and concerns.

When his father-in-law, Jethro, saw how exhausted Moses was, he admonished him that he would surely wear out. He offered Moses a wise suggestion—divide the people and delegate a group of leaders. Jethro advised him to appoint godly men to mediate the less significant disagreements, which would free Moses to handle major issues. Moses heeded his father-in-law's sound counsel and reduced his own burden.

Many pastors today struggle with fatigue and discouragement because they attempt to handle all the demands from their congregation. But the apostle Paul organized the early church with guidelines similar to Jethro's. Paul set up deacons as qualified pastoral helpers. We can take our concerns to them and let the pastor manage the weightier matters of the church. Divide and delegate—to support our church leaders.

Almighty God, we lift up our pastors to You. Help us remember to bless them while they bless us.

Holy Guidance

Pilate saw that he wasn't getting anywhere and that a riot was developing. So he sent for a bowl of water and washed his hands before the crowd, saying, "I am innocent of this man's blood. The responsibility is yours!"

MATTHEW 27:24 NLT

Pontius Pilate used the Jewish custom of hand washing to make it clear to the Jewish leaders that he would not accept responsibility for the wrongful death of an innocent man.

Because the unruly crowd repeatedly shouted for Pilate to crucify Jesus, he released Barabbas and handed over Jesus for execution. Pilate succumbed to mob pressure and, ultimately, fulfilled God's plan for the Lord Jesus Christ to die for our sins.

When we face difficult decisions that affect others, and peers crowd us with their desires like a pack of hungry wolves, do we capitulate to unreasonable demands? They frustrate us with their taunts, causing us to doubt our own discernment. Do we wash our hands of the situation and walk away? We have what Pontius Pilate didn't have—the guidance of the Holy Spirit. We can call on Him to quiet the din of the crowd and make it possible for us to resolve the issue in peace.

Abba Father, help us focus on You and seek Your guidance in our times of turmoil.

Consider. . .Then Respond

Then Moses raised his arm and struck the rock
twice with his staff. Water gushed out, and the
community and their livestock drank.

NUMBERS 20:11 NIV

Beaten down by constant complaints about the lack of water, Moses and Aaron fell on their faces before the Lord. God commanded Moses to speak to the rock to make it yield water as an unmistakable miracle from the Lord. The people's weak faith required yet another demonstration of His power.

Moses scolded the complaining Israelites, calling them rebels. Then he too rebelled. He struck the rock twice. God still provided, not because of disobedience but despite it. Water gushed forth for the people and their livestock. However, God denied Moses and Aaron the right to enter the Promised Land because of their disobedience. Although God forgave them, they bore the consequences of their sin.

How do we respond to wearying provocation and frustration? Our impetuous actions could embed a chasm between fellow believers and ourselves. And the consequences could cost us a loss of blessings. Let's take a deep breath and consider the Lord's instruction before fighting back.

O Holy God, teach us how to respond when
we are faced with provoking frustrations,
so that we may not dishonor You.

Increase in Knowledge

Without consultation, plans are frustrated,
but with many counselors they succeed.
<small>PROVERBS 15:22 NASB</small>

I penned my first novel with no knowledge about plot, characterization, and the acceptable style for a book. When I presented my finished work to an editor at a writers' conference, he explained, to my great disappointment, that the only correct part of my manuscript was the font. Rather than cave in to tears of frustration with so much to do, I chose to enroll in their fiction writing class.

In my zeal to be an author, I had failed to first consult with professionals, but I was open to instruction to improve my skills. Soon after the conference, I found a critique group with some published authors. They offered wise counsel, and with their direction and evaluation, together we helped one another grow and succeed. Now I have the privilege of offering my help to others.

We all need to consult with experts from time to time. The more skill we acquire, the more we increase in knowledge and proficiency, and the more we can encourage others. We can foster God's opportunities in their lives.

Almighty God, Wonderful Counselor, thank You
for removing our frustrations with an
abundance of counselors.

The Lord Remembers

Yet the chief cupbearer did not remember
Joseph, but forgot him.
GENESIS 40:23 NASB

No matter where Joseph went or what he did, the Lord prospered him, as well as those for whom he worked. Even while imprisoned for a crime he didn't commit, Joseph found favor with the chief jailer, who put him in charge. Then two new prisoners arrived: Pharaoh's cupbearer and baker.

Each man had a vivid dream they recounted to Joseph, who, with God's insight, analyzed and explained the dreams in detail. The cupbearer would be reinstated. The baker would be put to death.

Before the cupbearer was released and restored to his function in the royal court, Joseph asked him to plead his case before Pharaoh. But he forgot. Two years later, when the king had inexplicable, disturbing dreams, the cupbearer remembered Joseph. And Joseph was summoned.

Though being forgotten by man may have discouraged Joseph, the Bible records no complaints. In fact, Joseph seemed to have trusted the Lord so thoroughly that, no matter what, he knew the Lord was always with him.

People forget their promises to us, but the Lord remembers His until the end of time.

O Lord our God, thank You for Your everlasting
presence in our lives—in our prosperity
as well as in our distress.

Never Forsaken

And at the ninth hour Jesus cried with a loud voice,
saying, Eloi, Eloi, lama sabachthani? which is,
being interpreted, My God, my God,
why hast thou forsaken me?
MARK 15:34 KJV

As Jesus suffered a slow, excruciating death on the cross, He quoted Psalm 22:1. Besides the torturous physical pain, He experienced the abandonment of God as He bore all the sins of the world. Every sin—from the first bite of the forbidden fruit to the last sin that will ever be committed—fell on our perfect Savior. It must have broken the Father's heart to turn away from His only begotten Son at that moment.

Whatever we suffer, God fully knows our anguish. And as believers in Jesus Christ, we will never be forsaken. Even when we feel alone in our affliction, we will never know true abandonment. God is always with us. He had to desert Jesus on the cross so that He would not have to leave us—ever. That's how much He loves us.

Heavenly Father, in our human minds, we cannot
fathom the depth of Your sacrificial love for us.
You have made it possible for us to never have to
cry out to You, "Eloi, Eloi, lama sabachthani?"

A Way Out

Then both Mahlon and Chilion also died, and the woman was bereft of her two children and her husband.

RUTH 1:5 NASB

In the time of the judges of Israel, Elimelech of Bethlehem took his wife, Naomi, and their two sons to Moab to escape a famine. Elimelech died, leaving Naomi and their children destitute in a foreign land. She had no one to turn to except her boys, who felt the weight of profound sorrow in the death of their father.

Her sons married. Then they died.

These widows struggled to make ends meet, each grieving the loss of her respective husband. Naomi's grief was three times greater; she had lost a husband and two children. Although the women shared the burden of providing for themselves, concern for their future compounded Naomi's bereavement. But she faithfully trusted in God as she planned to return to Bethlehem.

God made a way out of this tragedy to bring forth the Savior. Ruth married a near kinsman of Naomi's and became the grandmother of a future king—David, son of Jesse, of the tribe of Judah and the lineage leading to Jesus.

Heavenly Father, as we grieve our own losses, let us trust in You to comfort and guide us.

Everlasting Arms

The LORD is near to the brokenhearted
and saves those who are crushed in spirit.

PSALM 34:18 NASB

The anguish of losing someone we love is indescribable. I've lost a mother, a father, a brother, and a beloved husband, each, in my humble opinion, too young to die.

But through our grief, we slowly learn to adapt to the loss and, in understanding its finality, adjust to a new routine. Our healing can take months or years.

After an unexpected death or the passing of a child, mourning may extend much longer. An overwhelming bereavement may produce such pervasive sorrow that a bleak depression settles in, blocking efforts to come to terms with the loss. To those crushed in spirit, the future seems hopeless.

But God's Word reminds us that we do have hope, no matter what life throws at us. Although death is inevitable, God still comforts us, heals our broken hearts, and lifts our spirits to embrace His merciful love. Let us lean on His everlasting arms in our grief.

Blessed God and Father, thank You that You have
allowed us to be born again to a living hope
through the resurrection of Jesus Christ.

Heaven's Joyful Gain

Brothers and sisters, we do not want you to be
uninformed about those who sleep in death,
so that you do not grieve like the rest of
mankind, who have no hope.

1 THESSALONIANS 4:13 NIV

When we cross from this mortal existence into eternal life, we receive relief from all the pain and misery of the flesh. We become whole again and gain perfect health and vitality—both physically and mentally—when the Lord calls us home.

Paul wanted the Thessalonian congregation to understand this truth. Since Jesus died and rose from the dead, we have the assurance that God will resurrect us as well. We will be in the amazing and glorious presence of the Lord forever. Knowing that we too will experience resurrection comforts us.

When we mourn a loved one, let us find comfort in our knowledge that our sad loss is heaven's joyful gain because of Jesus Christ's sacrifice. Our separation from the friend or family member through death is temporary. We will one day be reunited in God's family for eternity.

O Lord God, thank You for making it possible for us
to have hope in You during our period of mourning.
Reading Your Word keeps us tenderly wrapped
in Your matchless compassion.

The Great Healer

*He heals the brokenhearted
and binds up their wounds.*

PSALM 147:3 NKJV

Perpetual grief, also known as chronic sorrow, occurs during a long-term illness or after the loss of a body part. While death is final, a chronic illness can feel like infinity. Frustration follows in the wake of ongoing ailments.

With amputation or surgical removal of an organ, we mourn the lost body part. Sometimes phantom pain follows. While the rest of the body may heal, a lingering trauma remains. In some cases, our normal daily functions become difficult or impossible, and we need assistance to get through each day. This kind of humiliation saps our self-worth and leaves us vulnerable to depression.

Both grief and despair continue until we adapt to an altered lifestyle. Easier said than done by ourselves. But with the help of Almighty God, small steps toward healing physically, emotionally, and spiritually are possible. When we yield our sorrow to the Lord, He heals our broken hearts and binds our wounds.

God in heaven, You are the Great Healer. We give our pain, our sorrow, and our wounds to You and accept Your love, compassion, and mercy in return.

Solace of Humor

Laughter cannot mask a heavy heart.
When the laughter ends, the grief remains.
PROVERBS 14:13 TLB

When tragedy strikes, whether it's the death of a loved one, a natural disaster, or any other life-changing event, the solace of humor finds its way into our days of grief. God is lifting our heavy hearts, if only for a moment. We experience a respite from sorrow, a fleeting diversion from despair. The cushion of laughter reduces our tension, relaxes our responses, and lightens our outlook when we need it most.

A distressing loss leaves a hole in our hearts as well as our lives. Sharing amusing stories softens the edges of that painful cavity. But when the laughter fades, sadness returns. As we continue to recount our memories, the roles of sadness and laughter gradually reverse. Then we can visualize God's hand in the situation, and our tormenting "if only" thoughts slowly diminish.

If we let Him, the Lord will provide the cheerfulness we need to heal our aching hearts. We will laugh and smile and feel joyful again. . .soon. With God, it's possible.

Gracious God, please comfort our heavy hearts.
Give us laughter in our tears, joy in our sorrow,
and hope in Your loving embrace.

Give as Well as Receive

"Blessed are those who mourn,
for they shall be comforted."

MATTHEW 5:4 NKJV

While the Lord brings us comfort, He wants us to give as well as receive consolation. Jesus said if we do something for the least of these, His brethren, we have done it for Him.

When a friend mourned over her past sins, several of us reached out to her with sympathy and encouraging words. We reassured her that Jesus Christ paid for all her sins on the cross. Since He forgave her, then she could forgive herself. Our words helped lift her heavy heart.

When I mourned the loss of my job of ten years, family and friends reminded me that the hostile environment of the last year had strangled my joy. They assured me that the Lord had new and better plans for me. Without that stressful setting, I could write again.

Another friend mourned a broken relationship with one of her children. We comforted her with prayers, Bible readings, and loving hugs.

We pray for friends who bring the hope of the Gospel to the homeless, the chronically ill, and the imprisoned, supporting them in their difficult, yet rewarding, work.

Blessed Lord, grant us peace as we comfort one
another in our stressful situations.

Eternal Assurance

"LORD, reveal to me the end of my life and the
number of my days. Let me know how short-lived I am.
You, indeed, have made my days short in length,
and my life span as nothing in Your sight.
Yes, every mortal man is only a vapor."

PSALM 39:4–5 HCSB

King David knew he was dying. In this psalm, he didn't express fear of death but desired to know the date and time.

When my friend received a terminal illness diagnosis, her doctor gave her a year to live with treatment. She sought other medical opinions. They offered the same prognosis.

She and her family entered into the new realm of anticipatory grief. The symptoms of regular grief arrived early.

Like David, she didn't fear death. She had the assurance of eternal life. But the thought of leaving behind loved ones amplified her anguish. We did what we could to ease her trepidations, offering a sympathetic ear, a gentle embrace, and encouraging words. Scripture readings also brought some joy to her remaining time.

A year and a day after her diagnosis, she passed into the Lord's loving arms.

God has numbered our mortal days. Let us use the time we have left to honor Him.

Lord, comfort those in anticipatory grief. Our lives in this world are a vapor compared to eternity with You.

Debt Paid in Full

But if he has wronged you in any way or owes you anything, charge that to my account.

PHILEMON 18 NASB

Onesimus, Philemon's slave, had stolen from his master and run away to Rome. Providentially, he became acquainted with Paul, who brought him into the family of Christ. As a new believer under Paul's guidance, Onesimus served the Lord with faithfulness and devotion.

Paul couldn't keep another man's slave without the master's consent, so he admonished Onesimus to return in repentance—a dangerous choice. Punishment for an escaped slave was death, but Paul interceded on his behalf, offering to pay the debt the former slave owed. Philemon's well-known loving-kindness and help for the members of the small Colossian church gave Paul the confidence to send Onesimus back. He believed God would soften Philemon's heart.

We have that same confidence in our relationship with God. Although we deserved death for running away from God, Jesus Christ interceded on our behalf. He paid our debt—in full. And God softened our hearts and drew us toward our Savior.

God our Father, if we struggle to forgive someone for a deliberate offense against us, help us remember Your forgiveness for us through the sacrifice of the Lord Jesus Christ.

Heavenly Protection

Look upon my affliction and my trouble,
and forgive all my sins.
PSALM 25:18 NASB

David confronted his hardships and predicaments face-to-face. God had trained him and instilled courage through his early life as a shepherd, when he rescued his lambs from lions or bears. As a soldier and king, David took on greater challenges.

He grew to recognize the difference between self-imposed troubles and battles from his enemies. When he brought trouble on himself by caving to sin, he praised the Lord and sought His forgiveness. When distress came through his enemies, most of whom were also God's enemies, he praised the Lord and asked for deliverance. No matter what the situation, he exalted God and looked to Him for strength, protection, guidance, and mercy.

David offers us a wonderful example of trusting in the Lord. God protected him from Goliath, Saul, the Philistines, and even his son Absalom. He rescued David many times and restored his fellowship with Himself.

God sees our afflictions and troubles. He will protect us from our enemies and forgive all our sins if we come to Him and humbly ask.

Merciful Father, we turn to You when our troubles
afflict us. Deliver us from our distresses
and do not remember our sins.

Hope of Forgiveness

For I hope in You, O LORD;
You will answer, O Lord my God.
PSALM 38:15 NASB

As a result of his hurtful deeds, David's friends and family avoided him. Others betrayed him. His enemies sought to destroy him. To whom could he turn?

David confessed his sins, pouring out his heart to the Lord. Going beyond voicing his lament, he wrote out his acknowledgment of wrongdoing. His deep regret over his actions extended from his loved ones to God as the One he ultimately offended. David described God's burning anger like His hand pressing down on him, arrows sunk deep within the flesh, the indignation of foul and festered wounds. Yet he knew he could turn to the Lord and hold on to the hope of God's forgiveness.

When we grieve the Holy Spirit with our disobedience, He uses our conscience to rebuke us. We may suffer depression, anxiety, and even physical sickness when we harbor unconfessed sin. Like David, if we fully admit the wrong we have done, deeply lamenting our actions, we can anticipate God's forgiveness through the blood of Jesus Christ.

Father God, we come to You with heavy hearts
when we have sinned against You. We place
our hope of forgiveness in You.

Culture of Love

Help us, O God of our salvation, for the glory
of thy name: and deliver us, and purge
away our sins, for thy name's sake.
PSALM 79:9 KJV

In this psalm, Asaph begs God for help and deliverance from Israel's enemies and for forgiveness for the sins Israel's forefathers committed. They had adopted pagan worship and abandoned their love for the Lord and His commandments.

Asaph's plea reminds me to pray for my nation. The news tells us that hatred flows through our land like waters over Niagara Falls, wearying most of us to the point of sorrow.

The Lord provided a new nation for the early settlers of America to worship Him. Our forefathers, through the inspiration of the Holy Spirit, established a republic to ensure the people of their God-given rights. More recent office holders, either by choice or negligence over the years, have allowed corrupt government officials to dismantle those liberties. As we unconsciously pushed God's love away, Satan's hatred crept into the land. How can we turn the culture of hate into brotherly love? Only through prayer and godly behavior.

O God of our salvation, we lift up our nation in prayer
for a revival of Your love through us. Deliver us from
Your enemies, and cleanse us of our evil ways.

A Perfect Example

*Then said Jesus, Father, forgive them;
for they know not what they do.*
LUKE 23:34 KJV

Sometimes forgiving others for their offenses against us seems nearly impossible.... A confidence revealed in a gossip circle. A figurative knife stabbed in the back so deeply that it penetrates the heart. A lie shared to discredit good character. Verbal assault or physical battery intended to wound. Marriage vows shattered. How can we forgive people who intentionally cause so much pain?

Jesus told Peter to forgive not just seven times but seventy times seven. He wasn't offering a mathematical equation; He called for a new attitude that lets the offense go rather than harboring hurt. God doesn't number our offenses, and His mercies toward us are immeasurable.

When we hand over the situation to Him, God makes forgiveness possible. He knows why someone hurt us. When the damaging acts, statements, or attitudes break our fellowship with the offenders, we must forgive them and pray for them without holding a grudge—just like Jesus did.

*Father in heaven, thank You for providing the perfect
example of praying for those who wish us harm.
Jesus Christ asked You to forgive His
enemies from the cross.*

Trust Him

But Moses said to God, "Who am I that I should go to Pharaoh and bring the Israelites out of Egypt?"

EXODUS 3:11 NIV

Moses had a valid reason to fear returning to Egypt. While defending a fellow Hebrew, he had killed an Egyptian. Pharaoh learned of the incident and tried to execute him, but Moses escaped. He settled into the life of a shepherd in the land of Midian.

Then God called him to return to Egypt, where a death sentence awaited. Moses begged five times to be exempted from this vast undertaking. It would've been impossible for Moses to deliver his people from the grip of Pharaoh alone, but the God of his fathers promised to be with him.

We often search for an excuse when God calls us for His purposes. At first, all we see is our own view—the impossibility of the massive task. We know we can't accomplish it alone. But with God guiding our hands and feet, our thoughts and tongues, we can achieve anything for His glory. Moses trusted. God did it.

Hallowed Father, our I AM, who are we that You should choose us for Your purposes? We are Your beloved children, Your creation. When You call, help us respond, as Moses did, with "Here I am, Lord."

Confession

And Saul said to Samuel,
"But I have obeyed the voice of the LORD."
1 SAMUEL 15:20 NKJV

So David said to Nathan,
"I have sinned against the LORD."
2 SAMUEL 12:13 NKJV

Compare the actions of these two kings—Saul and David.

When Samuel presented evidence of disobedience, Saul blamed the soldiers in his army. Then he claimed they saved the enemy's best animals for a sacrifice. Was that truth or a failed attempt to ingratiate himself to the Lord? Because of Saul's unfaithfulness, God rejected him as king.

Conversely, David admitted his guilt when Nathan confronted him with the truth, and although he suffered the consequences of his actions, God forgave him. He established David's throne as the one through which He would bring in the Messiah. God referred to David as a man after His own heart.

Our decisions and actions can trigger wearisome circumstances. Do we emulate Saul, blaming others and making excuses? Or do we, like David, accept responsibility and humbly confess our guilt to the Lord? Following David's example brings God's forgiveness and, eventually, His peace.

O God, our Father, as we humbly confess our sins,
we thank You for Your long-suffering
patience and mercy toward us.

Heart Transformation

Then Ananias answered, "Lord, I have heard from many about this man, how much harm he has done to Your saints in Jerusalem. And here he has authority from the chief priests to bind all who call on Your name."

ACTS 9:13–14 NKJV

Ananias balked at the Lord's prompting to go to Saul of Tarsus in Damascus. After all, this man devastated the Jerusalem church, invading homes and hauling off Christians to be punished because of their faith. But now the Lord wanted Ananias to perform a merciful act for this cruel man: heal him of his blindness.

How is an evil heart transformed? Only through God's intervention. God chose Saul to bear witness of Jesus Christ to the Gentiles and Jews alike. As a Christian, Saul (renamed Paul) would suffer the same torments he had earlier perpetrated.

How is a victim's heart changed? Only God could persuade Ananias to show compassion to the man who persecuted, even killed, his fellow Christians. Ananias prayed and obeyed. He trusted God's assurance of Saul's genuine conversion.

Dear God, when You call on us to show compassion to an adversary, give us the courage to follow the example of Ananias: to pray then obey.

The Will of God

And He said to them, "My soul is deeply grieved to the point of death; remain here and keep watch."
MARK 14:34 NASB

Three times Jesus asked His disciples to remain alert and pray in the garden at Gethsemane. Each time they struggled to stay awake. Fatigued and emotionally drained, they couldn't comply. The disciples wanted to be obedient but failed.

Three times Jesus asked His heavenly Father to let the dreaded cup pass from Him. He prayed, "Abba! Father! All things are possible for You; remove this cup from Me; yet not what I will, but what You will" (Mark 14:36 NASB). God, in His righteousness and holiness, had to decline. A horrible fate awaited Jesus. As the sinless Son of God, He had to die to cancel the debt of sin for all humankind.

After receiving a no from God to His pleas, Jesus Christ, knowing the excruciating suffering He would bear, still accepted God's will. Unlike the disciples, He succeeded in obedience—even unto death.

Heavenly Father, we look to You for the strength
we need to be obedient to Your commands,
even when Your answer to our prayer is no.
Yet not our will but Your will, O God.

Willing Obedience

*And Hannah answered and said, No, my lord, I am a
woman of a sorrowful spirit: I have drunk neither
wine nor strong drink, but have poured
out my soul before the Lord.*

1 Samuel 1:15 KJV

Like other wives in the Bible, Hannah felt the anguish
of childlessness. Her husband treated her with love and
compassion, thinking that would alleviate her distress,
but even his kindness didn't replace her longing for
motherhood. She poured out her soul in fervent prayer
and vowed to the Lord to dedicate her firstborn son
to His service.

God delivered Hannah from a position of shame
to one of respect. She conceived and named the baby
Samuel, which means "name of God." After holding
her son, nursing him, and watching him grow, take
his first steps, and speak his first words, she kept her
vow. Hannah gave Samuel to Eli, the Levite priest, at
the temple. How difficult it must have been to keep
her promise.

The Lord honored Hannah's sacrifice and gave
her five more children to love.

When we think we have nothing left within us to
offer the Lord, He will provide His gift through our
own obedience to Him.

*Heavenly Father, open our hearts to be
sacrificially obedient to Your calling.*

Humble Confidence

*"And so I will go to the king, which is against
the law; and if I perish, I perish!"*
ESTHER 4:16 NKJV

Queen Esther suffered great distress when she learned of Haman's decree. He had convinced the king to destroy the Jewish population in and near Persia. Mordecai reminded Esther that the Lord had placed her in a royal status for such a time as this—to deliver her people from annihilation.

Queen Esther risked death by going before King Ahasuerus without first being summoned by him. He had not commanded her to appear before him in more than a month. Yet, this brave woman, internally strengthened by the Lord, approached his throne to plead for the lives of her people. Because of his love for Esther, the king extended his golden scepter, allowing her to advance with her request. Esther laid her life on the line in obedience to God to preserve His chosen people.

When we receive the Lord's blessing, He expects us to share with others. He wants to use us wherever we are to bring about His plan.

And because of God's love, we can come to His throne, without being summoned, with the humble confidence of Esther.

*Most Holy God, let us boldly draw near to Your
throne of grace in obedience to Your calling.*

Sharing Truth

"Be strong and very courageous. Be careful to obey all the law my servant Moses gave you; do not turn from it to the right or to the left, that you may be successful wherever you go."

JOSHUA 1:7 NIV

After Moses died, the Lord told Joshua to lead the Israelites across the Jordan to the Promised Land. He assured Joshua that He would be with him all the days of his life, and He directed him to do according to all the law that Moses had left him.

Adhering to God's statutes while surrounded by the rebellious multitude required great courage and obedience. God told Joshua that by faithfully keeping the commandments, he would find success wherever he went. Only by meditating day and night on the book of the law could Joshua fully obey.

We might have family members and friends who don't share our desire to know and obey God's Word. Their flippant, contrary attitudes frustrate us when we try to lead them to the Promised Land, our heavenly future. But as we read and study the Bible, we find the courage and strength to persist in sharing the truth so they can enter the family of God.

Loving God, we need Your strength and encouragement to obediently lead others from their wanderings and into our Promised Land.

Obedience. . .Always

But Peter and the apostles replied, "We must obey
God rather than any human authority."
ACTS 5:29 NLT

Multitudes of people became believers in the Lord
Jesus Christ because of Peter and the other apostles'
teaching at the temple. When the high priest and his
associates heard about their preaching, they put the
apostles in jail. Then an angel unlocked the gates and
let them go. He commanded that they return to the
temple and proclaim the message of eternal life.

Imagine the high priest's thoughts when he
learned his prisoners escaped locked gates and were
back again. Perplexing, to be sure. When the high
priest reiterated his orders for the apostles to stop,
they gave their oft-repeated response: "We must obey
God rather than any human authority."

We are expected to comply with our government's laws unless doing so means disobeying God.
How do we weigh one against the other? We choose a
fine or jail for violating the government, or we choose
God's wrath for disobeying Him. Peter and the apostles
took the beatings and imprisonment. They are heroes
of the faith.

O Holy God, through our history as a nation,
our lawmakers have chipped away at Your
commandments. Help us follow the obedience
of the apostles and always choose to obey You.

Safety in Numbers

And one standing alone can be attacked and
defeated, but two can stand back-to-back
and conquer; three is even better, for a
triple-braided cord is not easily broken.
ECCLESIASTES 4:12 TLB

A sheep separated from the flock makes an easy target. Hungry predators hide, camouflaged in the landscape, waiting for the opportunity to attack. The lone sheep grazes, despite the possible danger.

When we, like sheep, fall away from the fellowship of other believers, we become easy prey for our enemy. Peter tells us that our adversary, the devil, is prowling around like a roaring lion, seeking someone to devour. He watches for the solitary one who strays from the protection of the flock. If we stay together, we have safety in numbers.

The Good Shepherd will leave the ninety-nine to find the one missing sheep. We too can be watchful of our brothers and sisters in Christ. When we note absentees in our fellowship, we can contact them to make sure they are okay. And we can be more welcoming to those who slip in for a worship service and then leave unnoticed. Let us not neglect the fellowship of other believers.

O Lord, our Shepherd, help us stay ever watchful
for our predator and be mindful of any
missing sheep in our fellowship.

Gather in His Name

For where two or three are gathered together in my name, there am I in the midst of them.

MATTHEW 18:20 KJV

Jesus quoted the law from Deuteronomy when addressing the need for church discipline: "At the mouth of two witnesses, or at the mouth of three witnesses, shall the matter be established" (Deuteronomy 19:15 KJV). If an offender rejected the initial rebuke, Jesus advised the disciples to include one or two other believers in the reconciliation process, "that in the mouth of two or three witnesses every word may be established" (Matthew 18:16 KJV).

When discipline becomes necessary, Jesus encourages us to come together to pray for and counsel each other about deeds that need to be rectified. If prayer and guidance fail to persuade the offender, Jesus says that person must be removed from the fellowship of the congregation.

If we honor God's will in heaven by seeking what is best for His church, then we'll establish His will on earth.

When we gather in His name, even to rectify, Jesus is in our midst.

Our Father in heaven, we seek Your guidance and mercy when reprimanding our own. Thank You for giving us a Savior who is always with us.

Heavenly Focus

Then Jesus said to him, "Go your way; your faith has made you well." And immediately he received his sight and followed Jesus on the road.

MARK 10:52 NKJV

Hopelessly blind, Bartimaeus sat on the side of the road and begged. As Jesus approached with His disciples and the large crowd of people who followed Him, Bartimaeus called out to Him. Despite the harsh chiding from those nearby, he continued to shout. He acknowledged Jesus as the Son of David, the Promised One.

When asked what he wanted, Bartimaeus didn't waste the moment. He stated, "Rabboni, that I may receive my sight" (Mark 10:51 NKJV).

The cares of this world often blind us to what is important. Fixing our eyes on the latest fad, the newest techno-gadget, or fame and money, we unconsciously break our fellowship with the Lord. These worldly matters fail to satisfy us. In time, they lose their appeal, and we lose hope. Wearily searching for what we lost, do we have the same faith as that blind man on the road?

Bartimaeus believed the Lord could restore his sight, and when He did, Bartimaeus followed Jesus. Do we follow Jesus when He opens our eyes?

Gracious God, please help us focus our eyes on Christ, our Savior.

Shining Light

For it is God who is at work in you,
both to will and to work for His good pleasure.
PHILIPPIANS 2:13 NASB

Workday drudgery can wear us down. Day after day, week after week, an overbearing boss, an ill-tempered colleague, or a defiant subordinate can grind our resolve into dust. Sometimes it isn't our coworkers who drag us down but our job. Even an excellent career can result in overwork. Serving in emergency situations that require life-and-death decisions raises stress levels along with blood pressure and pulse rates. Weary and exhausted, we often feel frustrated and alone in our circumstances.

But we do not work alone. Our labor is in fellowship, hopefully with other Christians, but most assuredly with our Lord. As we acknowledge God working in us to endure the boss, the coworker, or the high-stress vocation, we reflect His light in our hectic world. When we strive to do our work without grumbling or disputing, we please God in our examples of Christlikeness.

Seeking the Lord's presence and His fellowship in our work through prayer, it's possible to keep on keeping on.

Almighty God, thank You for working in us
to help shine Your light in the busy world.

Unfathomable Peace

May you have more and more of His loving-favor
and peace as you come to know God and
our Lord Jesus Christ better.
2 PETER 1:2 NLV

The Lord created us for fellowship. As we get to know God through prayer and reading and studying His Word, we reflect His character and please Him. The apostle Peter listed Christlike qualities as moral excellence, knowledge, self-control, perseverance, godliness, brotherly kindness, and love. These define the nature of Christ in us.

Christ's shed blood washed away the stains of our immorality and rebellion. Knowledge of His Word helps us maintain self-control and resist temptations. Walking in His righteousness, we show brotherly kindness and love to each other. We are quick to forgive and eager to help.

Holding fast to these qualities in our daily lives draws us closer to the Lord. We will disappoint Him from time to time because we still struggle against fleshly desires. In those times, He offers His mercy when we humbly lay our failings at the foot of the cross. During both harmony and hardship, He fills us with His unfathomable peace.

Loving Father, please multiply Your grace
and peace in us as we make every effort
to know You more intimately.

Cling to God

*"Though He slay me, I will hope in Him.
Nevertheless I will argue my ways before Him."*
JOB 13:15 NASB

Despite the criticism from his friends, Job's only desire was to plead his case before Almighty God. He recognized that although God could put him to death, He could also deliver him. Fear would not prevent him from claiming his innocence in causing the tragedies that had befallen him.

Job's unyielding faith gave him confidence to approach God's throne of grace boldly, yet with humility. He asked God for only two things: to not abandon him and to communicate with him. He posed the question we often ask when suffering ongoing misery: "Why?" What atrocious sin had he committed to bring about these dire consequences? He had lived righteously before the Lord. Yet even in his wondering, Job believed that God would grant him mercy, vindicate his integrity, and end his suffering.

In his example of steadfastness, Job teaches us to cling to God. We may question as long as a trial endures, but our faith can remain strong.

Almighty Father, grant us mercy when we come to You in our suffering. Forgive us for questioning Your reasons. You are our best hope.

Hope of Resurrection

*For there is hope of a tree, if it be cut down,
that it will sprout again, and that the tender
branch thereof will not cease.*

JOB 14:7 KJV

Since the beginning of our existence, people have died and been buried, cut down like trees, seemingly without life. In his distress, Job compared man's life to a tree. A tree stump appears dead, but under the dirt, the roots seek nourishing water to restore life. In time, a tender shoot pops out of the ground in a different place.

Job believed death would release him from his suffering, but he asked, "If a man dies, will he live again?" (Job 14:14 NLV). He found hope in the coming resurrection. He could endure the agony, knowing that God would call him, and he would answer. Job's sin was no longer observable as God bound and sealed his transgressions.

And so it is with us. Jesus took our sin nature upon Himself to give us the hope of the resurrection. Like Job's tree, we will sprout again in the day of our resurrection, and our tender branches will never cease.

*Loving and merciful Father, thank You for planting
seeds within Your Word to give us hope of new life.*

Pray and Rejoice

Turn us again to yourself, O God of the armies of heaven. Look down on us, your face aglow with joy and love—only then shall we be saved.

PSALM 80:19 TLB

When the Assyrians captured the northern tribes of Israel, the people of Judah fell into dismal distress. Asaph cried out to the Lord, praying for not only a nationwide restoration but also a spiritual renewal. He put all his hope in the Lord.

As our nation spirals in moral and spiritual decline, with our enemies watching and waiting for us to fall, we have but one hope—almighty God.

When leaders of foreign countries rise up against us, we must drop to our knees in prayer. While others mock and look down on us, we lift our eyes to the Lord for guidance. Our foes within our borders scheme to cause dissension among citizens. We unite to stand strong in our faith in God.

We can find hope in Asaph's example and cry to the Lord for His deliverance. While others gnash their teeth, we will pray and rejoice in the Lord.

Dear God in heaven, we put our hope in You for deliverance from our enemies both within and outside our borders.

Future Hope

*The Spirit of the Sovereign Lord is on me, because the
Lord has anointed me to proclaim good news to the
poor. He has sent me to bind up the brokenhearted,
to proclaim freedom for the captives and release
from darkness for the prisoners.*

Isaiah 61:1 NIV

Isaiah gave hope to the people of Judah in his prophecies of the coming Messiah. He declared that those who mourn would be comforted. Praise would replace denigration. Instead of shame and humiliation, they would shout for joy. Vengeance and justice are always the Lord's.

When Jesus began His ministry in the synagogue at Nazareth, He stood in authority to read this portion of the book of Isaiah. He then announced that He had fulfilled the prophecy.

Isaiah predicted a future of hope. We look back to the finished work of Christ and His empty tomb for ours. He binds up our broken hearts. His sacrifice releases us from sin's grip. As the Light of the World, He dispels the gloom of hopelessness. We can rejoice greatly in the Lord.

*Lord God, as Isaiah gave hope to the nation of
Judah, let us claim our hope in the fulfillment
of his prophecies—Jesus Christ, our Savior.*

Overcomers

And hope does not disappoint, because the love
of God has been poured out within our hearts
through the Holy Spirit who was given to us.
ROMANS 5:5 NASB

Disappointment comes from many sources, like a broken promise, a rained-out summer vacation, or the latest gadget that doesn't live up to our expectations.

We may not always respond to disappointment the way the Lord wants us to. Instead we react without thinking. Pain may cause us to snap at others. But if we take a moment for a quick prayer—"Lord, how do You want me to respond?"—then through God's guidance, we can express His love and mercy. A calm demeanor produces a soft answer, and disappointment diminishes.

By seeking God's blessing when we face challenges, we overcome. As we press on, we develop perseverance and strength of character. Our hope emerges through our stalwart and faithful moral fiber.

People, places, and things are certain to fail us, but we can always count on our hope in the Lord to carry us past the disappointment.

Gracious heavenly Father, we exult in the hope
of Your glory as we carry on through
life's disappointing moments.

Hope Abounds

*Now may the God of hope fill you with all joy and
peace in believing, so that you will abound in
hope by the power of the Holy Spirit.*

ROMANS 15:13 NASB

The blessings of joy and peace come through our belief
in the Lord Jesus Christ. As the Holy Spirit indwells us,
we try to be like Christ in our attitudes and actions.
Jesus ministered to the Jewish people and the Gentiles,
to men and women, to rich rulers and poor servants.
He favored not one but all.

Treating our fellow men and women with love
and respect, regardless of their ethnicity or beliefs,
carries out the principles of brotherly love that Jesus
taught. When we are strong, we help the weak. From
our surplus, we provide for the needy. We feed the
hungry and tend to the sick or injured. We share the
message of Jesus Christ with the hopeless. God's
love shines through us so that we illuminate the path
to Him.

And as we give of ourselves, our hope abounds.

*God of our hope, thank You for granting opportunities
to show Your love through our giving. Let our joy
and peace through You bring hope to others.*

He Will Provide

*Now she who is a widow indeed and who has been left
alone, has fixed her hope on God and continues
in entreaties and prayers night and day.*

1 TIMOTHY 5:5 NASB

In biblical times, widows had few choices. Society
encouraged younger widows to either return to their
parents or remarry. Those who had families depended
on their relatives for support. The "widows indeed"
were older women, alone in the world, with no one
to provide for their welfare. Through prayer they
demonstrated their faith in God. Paul directed Timothy
to care for these women within the church.

When I placed my beloved husband into the arms
of the Lord, I became a member of the Order of
Widows Indeed. I had a job to cover my living expenses
. . .for a while. Then my employment ended, and as
a childless older woman, I felt isolated. Mortgage?
Utilities? Food? How could I manage without my
husband and without income? I fixed my hope on
God. Whether help comes from the church, friends, or
another job, I know He will guide and provide for me.

*Loving God, we who are widows indeed have fixed
our hope on You. We will continue in our
entreaties and prayers night and day.*

Unceasing Presence

"The LORD is the one who goes ahead of you;
He will be with you. He will not fail you or
forsake you. Do not fear or be dismayed."

DEUTERONOMY 31:8 NASB

Moses announced that Joshua would lead the Israelites across the Jordan River and into the Promised Land. Even with his proven track record, many hesitated to follow Joshua. Moses reminded them that the Lord would go with them, just as He did when they left Egypt and wandered forty years in the wilderness.

A shift in leadership paired with a significant change causes doubts. Even when a new leader has sparkling credentials, we still question if the change is a wise decision. We struggle with our misgivings. *Go. Stop. Wait.* But when the Lord affirms, "Go," the argument should end. He is the trustworthy Advocate.

We don't have the physical manifestation of God's presence in the pillar of fire by night or the pillar of cloud by day. But we do have His unceasing presence in us. No matter where we go, the Lord goes.

Father, our lives often consist of changes, and
sometimes decisions seem iffy. But knowing You are
ever present, we will not fear or be dismayed.

He Finds Us

He asked them, "What are you discussing so intently as you walk along?" They stopped short, sadness written across their faces.

<small>LUKE 24:17 NLT</small>

Three days after the crucifixion of Christ, a man named Cleopas and his companion walked toward Emmaus, a few miles away from Jerusalem. They discussed the disturbing news of what had happened to Jesus. In His resurrected body, concealing His identity, Jesus joined them on their journey. They all talked together. Jesus waited until later in the evening to open their eyes to see Him, and then He vanished.

Discouragement weighs us down in our own Emmaus experience. How often do we walk along in sorrow unaware that the Lord is with us on our journey? If we seek Him in our distress, He finds us. If we ask Him to show us the way, He will direct our paths.

Jesus reveals Himself to us in many wonderful ways. And, unlike the appearance to Cleopas, He won't vanish. He's here within us to stay.

Heavenly Father, we praise You for making it possible for us to walk with You in all our journeys. Let our hearts be glad and rejoice in Your faithful presence.

In His Hands

*So the king asked me, "Why does your face look
so sad when you are not ill? This can be
nothing but sadness of heart."*

NEHEMIAH 2:2 NIV

The remnant in Judah was in great distress. Nehemiah was profoundly saddened at this news. So King Artaxerxes questioned him. Nehemiah explained that his hometown of Jerusalem had been burned and left in ruins. He knew that this calamity came about because the people of Judah had sinned against God. He petitioned the Lord on their behalf.

Even today, people have been forced to leave their homelands because of dire circumstances. Some have been taken captive; others have fled because of oppressive political regimes, tribal wars, or corrupt leaders. In deep anguish, many have escaped without their possessions, abandoning friends and family members. The future must seem hopeless.

Like Nehemiah, we can petition the Lord for these people and their countries. As we pray for them, we can also ask God's protection over our nation. With God holding us in His hands, our future is filled with hope.

*God of heaven, we pray for displaced people
who are in anguish over their homelands.
Let them see Your mighty hand at work
to restore their faith and hope in You.*

Saved by Grace

*Then Peter remembered the word Jesus had spoken:
"Before the rooster crows, you will disown me three
times." And he went outside and wept bitterly.*

MATTHEW 26:75 NIV

*So Judas threw the money into the temple and left.
Then he went away and hanged himself.*

MATTHEW 27:5 NIV

Comparing these two men who betrayed Jesus, we see two different outcomes.

When all the disciples deserted Jesus, Peter took it one step further and denied knowing Him. Afterward, Peter was filled with regret and wept bitterly. He later received restorative mercy from the risen Lord on the shore of the Sea of Galilee.

In his guilt, Judas tried to return the thirty pieces of silver he received for handing Jesus over to the chief priests. Perhaps he had expected that Jesus would merely be arrested, not condemned. Filled with anguish, he thought he could never be accepted again by Jesus. So, he chose to kill himself.

We are all sinners saved by grace. No deed we commit is too evil for Christ to forgive. If we confess our sins, He is faithful and just to forgive us.

*Gracious Father, when we sin against You,
let us emulate Peter and come to You with
repentant hearts in the assurance that
Your forgiveness is always possible.*

Stop and Pray

And I said, Oh that I had wings like a dove!
for then would I fly away, and be at rest.
PSALM 55:6 KJV

The song "Somewhere Over the Rainbow" expresses young Dorothy's wish that she could fly to a place "where troubles melt like lemon drops." An evil woman planned to kill the girl's dog. Dorothy thought the only means to save her furry friend was to run away.

Did the composer know David's psalm about a traitorous friend who sought to kill him? David expressed his desire to fly away from his ally-turned-enemy, but he looked to God instead.

Fleeing from our problems rarely works. The trouble follows us or appears in another form, still waiting for a solution. Even in Oz, Dorothy's nemesis continued to pursue her.

When distress overpowers us, instead of wishing to fly over the rainbow, we should stop and pray. Like David, let us honor the Lord when we begin our prayer, then express our concern, and finish with our own assurance of God's faithfulness.

Great is the Lord, and greatly to be praised.
We seek You earnestly when our hearts are in anguish.
We give thanks to Your name, O Lord, for it is good.
For You deliver us from all our troubles.

Living Water

*"For thus says the LORD, 'You shall not see wind nor
shall you see rain; yet that valley shall be filled
with water, so that you shall drink, both you
and your cattle and your beasts.'"*

2 KINGS 3:17 NASB

Three kings from Israel, Judah, and Edom came together
against the Moabites. As they journeyed through the
wilderness toward Moab, they found no water for their
armies or cattle. One of the servants suggested they
inquire of the prophet Elisha. He instructed them to
dig trenches in the valley. They obeyed his directive.

Rain in the mountains of Edom then sent rivers of
water that flowed into the trenches. The armies and
their animals had more than enough to drink.

The Lord not only provided water but also used
that same water to confuse the enemy. The Moabites
thought it was blood, indicating vulnerability, so they
attacked prematurely. The three kings won the victory.

God's provision for us is His living water through
Jesus Christ. It flows through the trenches of our
hearts, sustaining us as we battle our adversaries.
When they see blood, it is the blood of Jesus, washing
away our sins and strengthening us.

*O Lord, You are our provision of living water
in every battle we face. We give You all the glory.*

Look Up

For the needy shall not always be forgotten;
the expectation of the poor shall not perish forever.
PSALM 9:18 NKJV

When we are weighed down by our troubles, we are robbed of a godly outlook on the future. We must lift our eyes from the murky situation and seek God's provision. Our focus can then shift from the despairing present to more hopeful prospects. We can also look back and remember the times when the Lord met our needs.

Jesus said that the poor would always be with us. Sickness, economic downturns, or broken relationships are only a few events that cause people to lose what they value. Some are a paycheck away from living on the streets.

There are many opportunities to minister to those who are less fortunate—or to receive help from those who have more than we do. God then works through us when we're able to give back.

Although our difficult circumstances might make us think God has forgotten us, He always remembers and provides for the needy. We have His Word on it.

To You, O Lord, do we lift our souls.
We put our trust in You to meet our needs.

Set Free

Who executes justice for the oppressed; who gives food to the hungry. The Lord sets the prisoners free.
Psalm 146:7 NASB

The psalmist gives us a plethora of reasons to praise the Lord. We can trust God, more than mortal man, for His many blessings and provisions.

God judges the wicked for oppressing His people. In our finite minds, we suspect they get away with their evil deeds through legal loopholes or corrupt officials. They scoff at the Lord, gloating in puffed-up arrogance at their apparent victory. But God's perfect justice has infinite consequences.

God feeds us not only with body-nourishing sustenance but also with His soul-nourishing Word. Jesus said that we will live not by bread alone but by every word that proceeds out of the mouth of God. The food we eat fills us for the moment, but God's Word lasts forever.

God liberates us from the prison of hopelessness. Held captive by the sin of Adam, we were doomed to separation from God. But He provided the sacrificial blood of Jesus Christ, which set us free to spend eternity in His glorious embrace. Only God could make this possible.

We praise You, O God, for Your everlasting provisions.

In Expectation

For He has not despised nor abhorred the affliction of the afflicted; nor has He hidden His face from him; but when he cried to Him for help, He heard.

PSALM 22:24 NASB

David learned at an early age to trust God. Even when it seemed his prayers fell to the ground, weighed down by his lamenting spirit, he knew the Lord would listen.

David was no stranger to discouragement. King Saul, consumed by murderous delusions, hunted him. David's own son conspired against him. The Philistines pursued him. His enemies came from all directions to attack him.

Through all his grievances and afflictions, David faithfully petitioned God for relief from his plight. He praised and honored the Lord in expectation of an answer. Many of his prayers included a confession of sin, in which he took responsibility for his strife. God heard and answered.

When we suffer various afflictions, let us come to the Lord with expectation. As children of the living God, we should be confident that our prayers soar to Him. He hears, and He answers.

Our loving Father, we praise You for Your loving-kindness. Forgive us where we have failed You, and deliver us from our afflictions.

Rock of Safety

*From the ends of the earth, I cry to you for help
when my heart is overwhelmed. Lead me
to the towering rock of safety.*

PSALM 61:2 NLT

Afraid and discouraged, David pleaded with the Lord for stamina and safety. He relied on his hope of God's faithfulness and on the assurance of His covenants, all of which inspired David to give glory and gratitude to God in advance.

In this psalm, David recalls earlier occasions when God had protected him and delivered him from his enemies. He never tired of calling on the Lord for help, and the Lord never stopped answering him.

We might experience moments when we think God says, *"Oh, not you again! What do you want now?"* That is a human response to repetitive cries for help, but not our heavenly Father's. His loving-kindness is part of His flawless character. He delights in our prayers and supplications as much as He treasures our obedience to Him.

Seek Him, and you will find Him. Ask, and it will be answered for you.

*Father God, You are with us in our most
disheartened moments as well as our most
joyous occasions. Quick to forgive and
slow to anger, You answer our prayers and
lead us to the towering rock of safety.*

Stilled Storms

Then they cried out to the LORD in their trouble, and he
brought them out of their distress. He stilled the storm
to a whisper; the waves of the sea were hushed.
They were glad when it grew calm, and he
guided them to their desired haven.
PSALM 107:28–30 NIV

Even the experienced sailors in this psalm struggled in
the face of a terrifying storm. As their ship climbed to
the top of the towering waves and plummeted down the
other side, they feared for their lives on the watery roller
coaster ride. But when they cried out to the Lord, God
hushed the storm, and the sea became tranquil. They
gave thanks to the Lord for His mercy and guidance.

Our rising swells aren't on tumultuous seas. The
ups and downs of a tragedy or distressing event in our
lives resemble a frightening storm. Our thoughts and
feelings are tossed about like a boat in a hurricane.

When we pray to God in our trouble, He will calm
our inner turmoil and will quiet the waves of our distress. He guides us to safety in His loving-kindness.
Let us remember God when the tempest is over.

We praise You, Lord, and give thanks for
You answering our calls of distress.

His Way, His Time

*In my distress I called to the LORD,
and He answered me. "LORD, deliver me
from lying lips and a deceitful tongue."*
PSALM 120:1–2 HCSB

Many of us have been harmed by lies and deviousness. Slander is a callous assault on the innocent party's character. Even when the truth exposes the treachery, the victim's integrity has already been damaged, sometimes to the point of humiliation and ruin.

What can we do when lying lips ignite the flame of gossip? Retaliation only serves two purposes: to drag us down to the level of the rumormongers and to exacerbate the hostile situation. Instead, we can follow the psalmist's standard and plead our case before the Lord. God hates a lying tongue, which is evil, untamable, and full of venom. In contrast, let us speak kind and loving words.

Trusting the Lord to vindicate our good name will bring us peace. God will answer our prayer and carry out justice in His way and in His time.

We present our trouble to You, Lord. Protect us from these falsehoods and deceptions. Because of who You are, Father God, we know You will answer our prayers.

Approachable God

On the day I called, You answered me;
You made me bold with strength in my soul.
PSALM 138:3 NASB

We don't have to be in distress to call on the Lord. He loves for us to come to Him in our times of joy as well. We can praise Him as we recall moments when He answered our prayers. How often has He exceeded our expectations with a multitude of blessings?

Each answered prayer emboldens us to come to God more frequently. Upon waking every morning, we can greet the Lord with thanksgiving for a new day and for watching over us during the night. We ask Him to bless our food at mealtimes. A news report will prompt us to pray for people we don't know or to praise Him for a good outcome in a life-threatening situation. As we prepare for bed, we can say, "Good night," and thank Him for all we accomplished that day.

Through the sacrifice of His only begotten Son, God has made Himself approachable. We are His children, and He delights in our bond with Him.

Heavenly Father, we thank You for answering our
prayers and praise You for making it possible for
us to come to You anytime, day or night.

Divine Purpose

*Then Hezekiah turned his face to
the wall and prayed to the Lord.*
ISAIAH 38:2 NASB

Isaiah brought a devastating report to King Hezekiah.
The king only had enough time to put his house in
order before his illness ended his life.

The king prayed fervently and wept in anguish.
He didn't try to bargain with God for a reprieve from
death but reminded the Lord how he had served Him
faithfully with a whole heart.

God heard his prayer and saw his tears. He sent
Isaiah back to tell Hezekiah he would be healed. The
Lord granted the king another fifteen years.

When we learned of my husband's illness, we wept
and prayed. He had served the Lord with a whole heart
too. The doctors said my husband could survive five
years with treatment. He lived only two. A friend's
grandmother received a terminal cancer diagnosis
at an early age. She told the doctor that, with ten
children, she didn't have time for cancer. She lived
another thirty years.

God answers our prayers according to His divine
purpose. We must use wisely the time He has already
given us.

*Eternal Father, when we don't understand how You
answer our prayers, help us remain strong in our
faith and continue to serve You wholeheartedly.*

He Rescues

But a messenger came to Saul, saying,
"Hurry and come, for the Philistines
have made a raid on the land."

1 SAMUEL 23:27 NASB

King Saul and his army pursued David throughout Judah with a fierce intent to kill him. The king had already overseen the slaughter of eighty-five priests who assisted David and his soldiers. Everyone in the province was afraid to offer them shelter.

David asked the Lord for guidance before he made a move.

Saul consulted his advisers, giving no thought to God's supremacy.

God warned David about an imminent betrayal, and David and his men fled from wilderness to wilderness, with Saul and his army in close pursuit. As the king's army surrounded them, a messenger arrived, shouting, "Hurry and come, for the Philistines have made a raid on the land." God's ways are truly mysterious.

Saul put his devious plot ahead of God's righteous plans. The Lord thwarted his mission.

David prayed, and God rescued him.

When our enemies surround us in an impossible situation, let us pray for guidance and protection, giving God the glory as He rescues us.

O Lord, You are the defense of our lives.
When faced with our enemies, we see
Your plan for us accomplished.

Source of Promise

Then Nathan the prophet went to Bathsheba,
Solomon's mother, and asked her, "Do you realize
that Haggith's son, Adonijah, is now the king and
that our lord David doesn't even know about it?"
1 KINGS 1:11 TLB

King David's son Adonijah usurped the throne while his father lay shivering on his deathbed. He didn't consult Zadok the priest, Nathan the prophet, or almighty God before declaring himself king. Adonijah unveiled his plan to eliminate other royal aspirants in his celebratory feast. Those not invited were marked for death, specifically Bathsheba and her son Solomon.

Bathsheba reiterated David's vow. She and Nathan both questioned the king about Adonijah's claim. King David publicly proclaimed Solomon as his successor to the throne. As Adonijah shrank back in fear, Solomon fulfilled the will of God.

In the same way that Bathsheba went directly to the source of the promise, we too can go to the source of our promises. As we encounter presumptuous adversaries, we know with all certainty that God's plans for us will not be hindered.

Almighty God, You have given us the promise of the
Holy Spirit, and through our belief in Jesus Christ,
we inherit the promise of Your unchanging purpose.

Yielding to God's Plan

"But the word of the Lord came to me, saying,
'You have shed much blood and have made great wars;
you shall not build a house for My name, because you
have shed much blood on the earth in My sight.'"
1 Chronicles 22:8 NKJV

King David made grand preparations to build the temple. He commissioned stonecutters, amassed bronze and iron, and acquired cedar logs from Sidon and Tyre. He wanted it to be a glorious tribute to the Lord, not for his own fame but to honor the God who had blessed him.

How disappointing God's denial must have been to David. Throughout his lifetime, he had praised the Lord with many psalms and prayers, but God said too much blood stained David's hands. God's plan was for Solomon to build the magnificent edifice.

Like David, we might have the best intentions when planning to serve the Lord. We make great efforts to prepare for a specific ministry, only to have our ideas struck down as an obvious no from God. The Lord has already chosen a "Solomon" to complete the task we had hoped to accomplish. Yielding to God's plan, we can accept His denial with the graciousness of David.

Our glorious God, please soften our hearts as
we comply with Your decisions, which You
planned even before we were born.

Glory. . .Forever

*For I consider that the sufferings of this present
time are not worthy to be compared with
the glory which shall be revealed in us.*

ROMANS 8:18 NKJV

My mother endured constant pain for thirteen years. Multiple surgeries on her spine and nervous system brought little to no relief. The agony must have felt like an eternity for her. It certainly did for us helplessly watching her suffer. The Lord released her from the bodily torment when He called her home to be with Him.

The apostle Paul understood pain and suffering; he survived beatings, snakebites, and shipwrecks. Keeping his focus on Jesus Christ, he didn't allow discouragement to overwhelm him. He considered his afflictions fleeting compared to the everlasting glory of God.

Our chronic sufferings are, in fact, temporary. I won my twenty-year battle with endometriosis through a surgical procedure. A special neck adjustment cured the immobilizing cluster headaches. Physical therapy spared me the same fate as my mother when I injured my spine—twice. God provided remedies in His own time.

Our physical bodies will give way to age, injury, or disease. But we are children of the Most High God, and our immortal souls will share His glory forever.

*Father God, help us focus on our future with
You as we endure our present sufferings.*

Sufficient Grace

Concerning this I implored the Lord three times that it might leave me. And He has said to me, "My grace is sufficient for you, for power is perfected in weakness." Most gladly, therefore, I will rather boast about my weaknesses, so that the power of Christ may dwell in me.

2 Corinthians 12:8–9 nasb

A recurrent ailment beleaguered the apostle Paul. We have no hint as to what his affliction was, only that God allowed it. Why would a loving God permit His faithful servant to suffer this perpetual thorn in the flesh?

It's easy for us to fall into the snare of pride and boasting when our efforts bring others to Christ. Our focus veers from working in ministry for the Lord to satisfaction in our achievements. Paul claimed his "thorn" kept him from self-exaltation.

Even though he implored God three times to remove the source of his misery, the answer remained the same: rely on God's sufficient grace. When neither prayer nor medical science can remedy our pain, perhaps the Lord is using it for His good purpose.

Merciful Father God, grant us Your grace and mercy as we humbly serve You, whether in pain or in contentment.

Comfort in the Scriptures

Your Word has given me new life.
This is my comfort in my suffering.
PSALM 119:50 NLV

When unsparing pain threatens to tear down our hope, we have the scriptures to encourage us. God's Word brings us closer to Him. As we read about the sufferings of God's servants (like Job, Joseph, Naomi, David, Paul, and others), we see Him working in and through each difficult circumstance. He disciplined, rescued, and upheld each of them for His higher purpose.

Job said he found consolation in not denying the words of the Holy One. In this psalm, David affirmed that God's life-giving words consoled him in his most despairing moments. Paul wrote that whatever was written in ancient times was written for our instruction to help us persevere. In his letter to Timothy, he stated that all scripture is beneficial for instructing, reprimanding, refining, and preparing us.

And no one suffered more than Jesus Christ, yet He quoted Psalm 22 during His agony on the cross.

Even in our unrelenting pain, we can find comfort in reading the Bible, memorizing significant verses, and praying God's Word back to Him.

O Holy God, we trust in You. Revive us through Your righteousness and comfort us with Your sacred words.

Sharing God's Love

Then they sat down on the ground with him for seven days and seven nights with no one speaking a word to him, for they saw that his pain was very great.

JOB 2:13 NASB

Job's three friends, Eliphaz, Bildad, and Zophar, meant well when they accused him of bringing his tragedies on himself. They claimed he needed to get his heart right with the Lord. A despairing man expects kindness from his friends, but Job received rebukes. He admonished them to do their own soul searching as they showered him with "proverbs of ashes" (Job 13:12 NASB) in their windy words.

I have shoved both feet into my mouth when trying to console friends in need. In my attempts to encourage them, I offered statistics about the illness or injury, or I described how the situation could've been worse. My efforts didn't help.

We try to comfort our loved ones, but our windy words often get in the way. Our friends in need only desire a strong shoulder to cry on or someone to sit quietly with them and hold their hands.

Loving God, please give us a strong shoulder, soft words, and a tender touch to show our dear ones Your merciful love.

Restored

For the Lord will not cast off forever. Though He causes grief, yet He will show compassion according to the multitude of His mercies. For He does not afflict willingly, nor grieve the children of men.
LAMENTATIONS 3:31–33 NKJV

Jeremiah wept for Jerusalem because the people had greatly sinned against God. They turned away from Him, abandoned His laws, and worshipped pagan idols. Their contempt brought judgment from the Lord. As punishment, the Babylonians would destroy the city and the temple. They would take the people of Judah captive and send them to Babylon. Jeremiah tried to warn them, but no one would listen to him.

God's righteousness calls for discipline when, as individuals or as a nation, we willfully walk away from Him. He doesn't delight in our grief but looks on us as a heartbroken father views beloved, wayward children. They must be punished for their defiance or they won't learn to walk in obedience. But when we return to the Lord in genuine repentance, He will show His compassion and restore us to Himself.

Merciful Father, we have rebelled, individually and nationally, against You and Your laws. We pray for hearts to be changed to honor and love You.

A Healing Balm

This change of plans greatly upset Jonah,
and he became very angry.

JONAH 4:1 NLT

Jonah boiled with anger when he realized that God planned to spare the Ninevites because they repented. These brutal people had perpetrated the most cruel and heinous acts against the Israelites. Jonah preached to only a third of the Ninevites. How could they so easily turn from their evil ways? How could God extend His mercy to them?

Jonah felt more compassion for the plant that provided him shade than he did for the entire population of Nineveh. But God wanted to spare those wicked people from an eternity without Him.

Each of us has our own Ninevites, enemies who rain troubles on us to the point of despair. Praying for God's blessings on our adversaries might be the most difficult emotional task we will ever perform. But that is exactly what the Lord commands us to do. Jesus said to love our enemies and pray for those who persecute us. Praying for their repentance and sharing God's compassion toward them is a healing balm for our peace of mind.

O God, our Father, forgive our bitterness and anger
toward our enemies. Soften our hearts so that we
can rejoice in Your compassion toward them.

Power of God's Word

Seeing the people, He felt compassion for them,
because they were distressed and dispirited like sheep
without a shepherd. Then He said to His disciples,
"The harvest is plentiful, but the workers are few."
MATTHEW 9:36–37 NASB

So great was His compassion for His people that Jesus sent His disciples to the lost sheep of Israel first. He provided the men with His healing powers and authority over unclean spirits to further their ministry. But they were not to go to the Gentiles or the Samaritans yet.

Our compassion for the unbeliever's fate begins with our family. Then we extend our ministry to friends, neighbors, and strangers we meet through daily activities. The Lord doesn't grant us the powers that He gave the disciples, but we have the power of His holy Word to share.

It's easy to feel frustrated and weary when people reject the message of eternal life. Why don't they see Christ's light shining through us? Perhaps they choose to wear blinders, like horses, to keep them unaware of truth surrounding them. Heartbreaking as it is, we can continue to extend our compassion to them not with words but with our Christ-honoring conduct.

Precious Lord, as we express Your compassion for
the lost sheep in our lives, help us proclaim
that Your kingdom of heaven is at hand.

Shared Joys and Sorrows

Rejoice with them that do rejoice,
and weep with them that weep.
ROMANS 12:15 KJV

Empathy, *kindness*, and *concern* are only a few synonyms for the word *compassion*. The statements "I'm sorry for your loss" or "I'm happy for your good news" might be polite, but they don't truly express compassion.

The example of empathy that Paul offered to the church in Rome teaches us to actually share each other's joy or grief to prove our true love for God. Sharing means taking a partnership or joint tenancy in the event. When we empathize with others, we invest ourselves in their lives.

God invested Himself in us when He created the first man. Jesus invested Himself in us when He paid the penalty for our sins. Paul invested himself in us when he risked his health and life to spread the Gospel throughout his world.

When a phantom wave of grief overcame me, my friend offered tea, chocolate, and sympathy. Later, when she lamented over a family misfortune, I comforted her. We have since shared the joys of her new grandbaby and my new writing opportunities.

Our compassion proves our investment in each other as God commanded.

Gracious God, thank You for teaching us about
compassion as we rejoice with those who
rejoice and weep with those who weep.

Gracious Compassion

*He comforts us in all our affliction, so that we may be
able to comfort those who are in any kind of affliction,
through the comfort we ourselves receive from God.*

2 CORINTHIANS 1:4 HCSB

As a child, my brother enjoyed setting up dominoes on his bedroom floor. He created intricate designs that snaked throughout the room, under the bed, and into the closet. Tapping the first domino initiated the cascading effect of each falling and touching the next one in turn.

And so it is with comforting others who suffer various afflictions. Hardships we endure are opportunities to demonstrate God's grace through us. The Lord deems us His first domino. As He comforts us with His loving touch, we can then reach out to others with compassion. He sets the domino effect in place to spread His comfort.

I didn't know how to comfort a widow until I lost my husband. God still upholds me in His merciful and gentle arms as I minister to other widows. And now they can console other women in bereaved circumstances. Each life we touch in Christian love expands God's gracious compassion.

*Merciful Father, thank You for our afflictions that
give us Your insight into bringing comfort to others.
Grant us the willingness to be Your first domino.*

Bear Another's Burden

Bear one another's burdens,
and thereby fulfill the law of Christ.
GALATIANS 6:2 NASB

In his letter to the Galatians, Paul addressed the issue of a fellow Christian being caught in sin. He encourages us to restore that person with a spirit of compassion. The extra burden of confession and repentance is often too heavy a load for some to bear alone. When God convicts a person of sin, the Holy Spirit groans within them to make them aware of right and wrong. We can lighten the burden for them by offering our prayers, help, and support.

A multitude of stuffed bears in different sizes adds a whimsical ambiance to my home. Aside from their cuteness and sentimental value, each one reminds me to bear another person's burden and pray for the one in need or suffering under the oppressive weight of his or her conscience. The gentle reminders greet me every day. As I respond to their presence, the Lord encourages me to fulfill the law of Christ, which is to love each other as we love ourselves.

Our Holy Father, give us the willingness to bear
each other's burdens with compassionate hearts.

Our Consolation

*"Then I would still have this consolation—my joy
in unrelenting pain—that I had not denied
the words of the Holy One."*

JOB 6:10 NIV

Job pleaded with God to take him, to let him die and
be at peace. He had lost his appetite for food, as well
as his will to carry on with life. Adding insult to injury,
his friends pelted him with rocks of accusing words.
He weighed his afflictions against the comments from
Eliphaz, Bildad, and Zophar, wondering which was
heavier. His friends presumed in error that Job had
an unrepentant attitude toward God, which caused
his calamities.

In all his suffering, Job remained faithful to the
Lord. Despite his friends' apathetic charges against his
character, he held tight to his belief that God would
relieve him of his blight either by healing or by death.

When we are in the middle of an impossible adver-
sity such as a natural disaster, sickness, or the death
of a loved one, the only stability is in our foundational
trust and belief in the Lord. Our faith in Him will be our
consolation as He lovingly guides us through hardship.

*Loving Father, as we suffer unrelenting pain
or emotional anguish, let us find joy in our
faithfulness to You and Your holy words.*

He Is Faithful

*Great is his faithfulness; his loving-kindness
begins afresh each day. My soul claims the Lord
as my inheritance; therefore I will hope in him.
The Lord is wonderfully good to those who
wait for him, to those who seek for him.*

LAMENTATIONS 3:23–25 TLB

The prophet Jeremiah proclaimed his inconsolable despair at the destruction of Jerusalem. The Lord pronounced His fierce judgment on the city's inhabitants because they rejected Him. They continued in their idol worship in the face of starvation and the threat of invasion.

Jeremiah had warned them repeatedly, yet they ignored his good counsel. He suffered their fate with them. Then Jeremiah remembered God's goodness to those who waited for Him and sought Him. He had hope in the Lord's faithfulness and mercy.

God looks at our hearts then distributes His judgments and blessings accordingly. When we come to Him in humble repentance, we can count on His faithfulness to forgive us. Through His loving-kindness, He restores us as a new day, fresh with opportunities to serve Him. No matter how dismal our circumstances might be, God is faithful to us.

*Merciful God, great is Your faithfulness!
As Your loving children, we put our hope
in You for our blessings and disciplines.*

A Mighty Advocate

*But the Lord is faithful, and He will strengthen
and protect you from the evil one.*

2 THESSALONIANS 3:3 NASB

In Paul's cautionary letter to the Thessalonian Christians, he asked them to pray for Silvanus, Timothy, and himself. They had encountered spiteful and depraved men who perverted the truth of Jesus Christ regarding the pending day of the Lord. This doctrinal misinterpretation called for prayer and discipline.

Paul reminded the Thessalonians of God's faithful guardianship of His church, the body of believers. The Lord would give them the strength they needed to reprove the false teachers, and He would shield them from demonic retaliation.

Some congregations today strive against flaccid or misleading doctrine. It seems impossible for us to correct the erroneous principles, especially when the teacher or preacher has a theology degree and we don't. But we have a mighty Advocate, One who requires us to teach His truth. Because of God's faithfulness to us and our faithfulness to Him, He will grant us the spiritual strength and protection we need to complete this task for Him.

*Righteous Father, please give us the power and
confidence to instruct the teacher with gentleness
and reverence. Direct our hearts to the
steadfastness of Your faithfulness.*

Our God Is Greater

Beloved, while I was making every effort to write you about our common salvation, I felt the necessity to write to you appealing that you contend earnestly for the faith which was once for all handed down to the saints.

JUDE 3 NASB

Concerned about Gnostic intruders in the church, Jude, the half brother of Jesus, wrote to encourage the Christians in their faithfulness to the Lord. Unbelievers had deviously joined the church for the sole purpose of misleading the followers of Christ.

Since Gnostics alleged that all material things were evil and that everything spiritual was good, they denied Jesus as the Sovereign Lord—God in the flesh. With their flattering words, these godless men attempted to promote errant doctrines. But Jude's letter enlisted an army of faithful Christians to refute their deceptions.

The evil one has besieged our churches today. He sneaks unholy intruders in among the believers. We prove our faithfulness to the Lord when we stand firm in our belief in Jesus Christ as the only begotten Son of God and in the truth the beloved saints bequeathed to us. Satan cannot defeat our army of faithful Christians, for God is greater than an angel.

All-powerful God, our Father, please keep us from stumbling as we earnestly contend for the true faith.

Timely Deliverance

These proud men who hate your truth and laws have dug deep pits for me to fall in. Their lies have brought me into deep trouble. Help me, for you love only truth. They had almost finished me off, yet I refused to yield and disobey your laws.

PSALM 119:85–87 TLB

In several psalms, we read about the enemies who dug pits, set traps, and hid snares to catch the faithful believer. Each psalm provides a prayer for God's rescue or deliverance and almost always includes praises for God's mercy.

As Christians, our enemies are Satan, who is the craftiest of all God's creatures, and his fallen angels. They know how to set human beings as rivals against each other and how to goad unbelievers into setting traps or deep pits to catch us in a sinful act. Persecution often includes false accusations or other deceptions to disparage and mutilate our good reputations.

If we remain faithful to God's Word and seek Him daily in prayer, He will rescue us in His own way. Our enemies could trip over their own obstacles and fall into the pits they've dug for us. Or their lies and other shams will fizzle out like a flame deprived of oxygen.

Heavenly Father, we wearily struggle against persecution from Your enemies. We praise You for Your timely deliverance and mercy.

Unstoppable Blessings

*"Blessed are those who are persecuted
for righteousness' sake, for theirs is
the kingdom of heaven."*

MATTHEW 5:10 NKJV

Jesus knew the persecution of His followers would begin soon after His death and resurrection. It began with Peter and John when they healed a lame man. Then a young, uneducated layman named Stephen amazed the men in the synagogue with his wisdom. He became the first martyr for his faith in Jesus Christ. Saul of Tarsus hounded and harassed Christians until he became a bondservant of Christ. He then suffered the hounding and harassment for the sake of righteousness.

The evil one will try to counter our blessings with his "stressings." When we begin our work for the Lord, for His righteousness, Satan will try everything in his angelic power to stop us. But we have the all-powerful Holy Spirit to help us through these seemingly impossible times of persecution.

God prepared His kingdom for us from the foundation of the world. He knew then that we would suffer for doing good now. The Lord will honor us with His many unstoppable blessings in the future.

*Blessed Father, we have the hope of Your promised
kingdom of heaven as we endure the temporal
persecutions the enemy aims at us.*

Soft Hearts

Bless those who persecute you;
bless and do not curse.
ROMANS 12:14 NASB

Peter and John prayed for their persecutors after being jailed for healing a lame man. Stephen prayed for God to forgive his murderers as they stoned him to death. Paul had to forgive himself for his earlier persecution of Christians so that he could bless those who sought to mistreat or kill him.

Our natural tendency is to curse those who persecute us. We want to retaliate and give them a taste of their own medicine. But God commands us to bless them. Jesus said to offer them our other cheek when they strike us. Loving those who love us is easy. Can we love those who hate us? When we respond with kindness in our hearts, they might be subjected to their own shame and remorse. How better to reach them with the Gospel of Jesus Christ!

Paul admonishes us to let our love be without hypocrisy. Cursing our enemies does not express God's love. When we tell ourselves it's impossible to ask God to bless our persecutors, let us pray for God to soften our hearts, as well as theirs.

Dear God in heaven, let Your words be our words
when those who hate You come against us mightily.

Do Not Be Troubled

But even if you should suffer for the sake of righteousness, you are blessed. And do not fear their intimidation, and do not be troubled.

1 PETER 3:14 NASB

In his admonition to Christians to fear God and not man, the apostle Peter quoted God's words to Isaiah. In Isaiah's day, the people of Judah feared the Assyrians. In Peter's day, the Christians feared the Romans. The pagan society in Rome persecuted Christians through intimidation. Their hostility grew as believers continued to live faithfully for the Lord. Peter emphasized the sanctity of Christ the Lord as their source of hope in the harassment they suffered.

Today, evildoers mock and disparage our good deeds, which we carry out for the Lord's objectives. Their goal is to bully us into withdrawing in fear. As Peter and Isaiah both stated, we must fear God and not man. Whatever humankind might subject us to in this lifetime, we have the promise of eternal blessings from our Father in heaven. Let us hold on to that hope so we will not be troubled.

Almighty God, give us courage when we face intimidation, for we do not face it alone. You are with us.

Godly Living

Indeed, all who desire to live godly
in Christ Jesus will be persecuted.
2 Timothy 3:12 nasb

In his letter to Timothy, Paul referred to the dreadful persecutions he and Barnabas endured in Antioch, Iconium, and Lystra. The Gentiles rejoiced and glorified the Lord when Paul and Barnabas explained the Gospel. But the Jewish leaders drove them out of the district.

In Iconium, a large number of Jewish people and Greeks accepted the Gospel. Then the unbelievers stirred up resentment, with threats to stone Paul and Barnabas.

In Lystra, the Jewish leaders came from Antioch and Iconium. They stoned Paul then left him for dead on the outskirts of town. But he got up and went back into the city.

Even in our modern day, we Christians aren't free of vicious persecutions. A young woman in the Middle East brought her suitcase, packed with all her belongings, to her baptism. She had to flee as soon as the pastor brought her out of the water. Her family had pronounced a death sentence on her. Through her tribulation, her fate is set: she will enter the kingdom of God because she desires to live godly in Christ.

Lord God, grant us the strength and courage we need
to live godly in Christ Jesus, especially in persecution.

The Good News

*Do not be surprised, brothers,
if the world hates you.*

1 JOHN 3:13 HCSB

Cain killed Abel out of hatred for his brother's righteousness. This demonic hatred for God's obedient children has been passed down through the centuries.

Jesus predicted that we would experience persecution for His name's sake. Scorn often hovers over those who pray in public places, such as sporting, political, or public school events. Christian business owners are engaged in legal battles for taking a stand on worldly issues that are contrary to God's Word. Bosses might surreptitiously discharge employees who display Christian values through their actions or speech. Missionaries in other countries must hide from satanic militant leaders who will imprison, or even execute, them if they dare to whisper the name of Jesus Christ.

Satan is the father of all lies and hatred. He seeks to defame, discredit, and destroy us because he envies our personal relationship with our Creator. Through the sacrificial blood of Jesus Christ, God has snatched us out of Satan's hand of eternal death and cradles us in His gentle arms of everlasting life.

Yes, the world hates us, but the good news is God loves us.

*Loving Father, thank You for Your gift of everlasting
life and Your eternal love as we endure
the hatred of the fallen world.*

Sound Counsel

For You are my rock and my fortress; therefore,
for Your name's sake, lead me and guide me.

PSALM 31:3 NKJV

David proclaimed that his faith in the Lord was a shelter from his enemies. He petitioned God to hear his prayer and rescue him. He knew from past experience that God would guide him away from the snare they had set for him. In his distress, David trusted the Lord to deliver him from the hands of those who pursued him.

Like David, we can trust the Lord to lead us away from the enemy's traps. But we must be willing to follow Him. We stumble into Satan's dodgy pits when we aren't paying attention to God's warnings. He wants us to be alert and on guard so He can guide us to His sheltering arms.

In distress or doubtful moments, the Lord will be gracious to us. We can depend on His sound counsel as we pray and meditate on His holy Word. He is our rock of strength and our fortress.

In You, O Lord, we take refuge. Let us rejoice in Your
righteousness as You deliver us from the enemy and
guide us to the haven of Your loving-kindness.

Devoted

Search me, O God, and know my heart; try me and know my anxious thoughts; and see if there be any hurtful way in me, and lead me in the everlasting way.
Psalm 139:23–24 NASB

David asked God to assess his motives in this self-reflective psalm. After glorifying God for His omniscience and omnipresence, David prayed for the Lord to judge the wicked men of bloodshed. Those men had desecrated the name of the Lord. In his faithful devotion, David believed that anyone who reviled the Lord was his enemy too. He reaffirmed that God would lead him in the eternal way. The way of the wicked is mortal, for they will perish.

What will God find when He searches our hearts? Are our motives as pure as David's when asking Him to judge the wicked? Can God lead us when there's bitterness in our hearts?

God will keep our anxious thoughts from clouding our vision so we can follow Him.

This psalm of David comforts us as we affirm our devotion to the Lord.

Everlasting Father, we implore You to search us, try us, and lead us. Let our thoughts not be veiled in a cloud of uncertainty. Give us clarity of mind, purity of motive, and hearts filled with Your love.

Right Paths

Trust in the LORD with all your heart, and do not rely on your own understanding; think about Him in all your ways, and He will guide you on the right paths.
PROVERBS 3:5–6 HCSB

When we're faced with insurmountable obstacles in life, it seems the last thing we do is trust God to handle them for us. We rush around, our minds filled with worry, searching for solutions. We can fix our dilemma by ourselves, right? Maybe not. Sometimes it isn't until we crumble under the weight of the trouble and land facedown in a puddle of our tears that we consider going to the Lord in prayer.

We serve an incomparable God, a doting Father, who loves us with an everlasting love. Through our faith in Jesus Christ, we have fellowship with Almighty God. He won't shove us to the side, no matter how gigantic or miniscule our challenge may be. Nothing is too big or too small for Him. He will give us clear instructions to remove the obstacles and will guide us through for His purposes.

O Lord, remind us to trust in You first when impossible situations overwhelm us. We will follow Your guidance to the right paths.

91

Peaceful Embrace

In peace I will lie down and sleep, for you alone,
LORD, make me dwell in safety.
PSALM 4:8 NIV

Confident that the Lord heard and answered his prayer for protection, David felt secure. God had shown him favor against his enemies. He could rest and sleep soundly with the assurance that the Lord watched over him.

Every night when I go to bed, I ask the Lord to watch over the members of my household while we sleep. When we wake up in the morning, I pray and thank the Lord for bringing us safely through the night to enjoy the blessings of a new day.

The few nights that I suffer with insomnia, the sleeplessness is rarely from fear or worry about my safety. My busy mind stubbornly hangs on to events of the day, or a hectic outing renders me too tired to sleep. On those occasions, I go to the Lord with prayers for my ailing friends and family, for my nation, for the protection of first responders and military personnel, and for salvation for loved ones who don't believe in Jesus. Like David, I feel God's peace embrace me as I drift off to sleep.

O God, our Protector, tuck us into bed to
lie down in peace and sleep, for You
alone can make us dwell in safety.

Trust. . .Forever

The LORD also will be a stronghold for the oppressed,
a stronghold in times of trouble; and those who know
Your name will put their trust in You, for You, O LORD,
have not forsaken those who seek You.

PSALM 9:9–10 NASB

David described God as a stronghold, an impenetrable citadel. In ancient times of war, the enemies would crash through the gates of a castle with battering rams. How frightening that must have been for those who sought safety inside the fortified walls. The enemy had breached their last bastion of hope. But God is our mighty fortress. We have no need to fear. With one gust of His breath, He turns the battering ram into sawdust. The almighty power of our Lord stuns our oppressors.

We who know God through His Son, Jesus Christ, can trust in His protection. He has provided us with a haven in His name. We pray. He answers. We praise Him. He embraces us. He abides with us forever and will never forsake or forget us in times of trouble or in times of comfort.

We praise You, Lord, for being our stronghold
against our oppressive enemies. We will
put our trust in You forever.

He Knows Your Heart

The LORD replies, "I have seen violence done to the
helpless, and I have heard the groans of the
poor. Now I will rise up to rescue them,
as they have longed for me to do."
PSALM 12:5 NLT

Where can we turn when people assault us with their
slanderous lies? Although they are not physical attacks,
these falsehoods are verbal attacks on our character.
God calls them acts of violence on the helpless because
they can devastate a person's livelihood. Instead of
communicating truth, the wicked manipulate it into
lies for their own selfish measures.

The Lord sees the damage these evildoers cause
with their deceitful, empty talk, and He hears our
earnest prayers. We can trust His promise to deliver
us in His time and in His way.

Where can we turn when people assault us with
their slanderous lies? We can always turn to our Lord
in prayer, for He will rescue us and protect us as we
endeavor to clear our names. Whether or not we can
prove our innocence, God knows the truth about us.
He knows our hearts. And He knows theirs as well.

Rescue us, O Lord, when our good names are
smeared. We turn to You, trusting in
Your promise of deliverance.

You Belong to Him

The LORD is my rock, and my fortress, and my deliverer;
my God, my strength, in whom I will trust; my buckler,
and the horn of my salvation, and my high tower.

PSALM 18:2 KJV

David listed many symbols to describe God's protection: An unyielding rock. An impassable fortress. A buckler, which is a protective shield. The horn of salvation, which is a powerful defensive weapon. And a high tower, which is an inaccessible sanctuary. God's protection is unfailing!

David rejoiced in God's deliverance of him from King Saul and his soldiers. Many times he had smelled the foul breath of death and asked the Lord for help.

God heard each prayer, and each time, He delighted to come to David's rescue because of his loyal obedience. David always gave God credit for saving him and strengthening him for yet another battle. He praised God for making his enemies turn and run, for protecting him from the strife of the people, and for executing vengeance for him as the anointed king.

We too can rejoice in God's protection, even while we wait for Him to deliver us from our enemies. We know He will rescue us—because we belong to Him.

O God, our rock and our fortress, we praise
You today for our deliverance tomorrow.

Our Shepherd

*Yea, though I walk through the valley of the shadow
of death, I will fear no evil: for thou art with me;
thy rod and thy staff they comfort me.*

PSALM 23:4 KJV

Sheep can smell a predator in a valley or pasture. They turn toward the wind to sniff for danger. When they sense it, what can they do but fear? They have no means of defense and must rely solely on their shepherd for protection. The shepherd's rod is for fending off wild beasts, and he uses the staff, or crook, to guide wandering sheep back to the safety of the fold.

We are the sheep of the Lord's pasture. When our predators close in on us, we look to our Shepherd for protection. God defends us against their vicious attacks with His rod of righteousness.

When we roam away from the flock and into the path of our enemy, God guides our wayward feet back to the safety of His fold with the staff of His holy Word.

We find peace and comfort in the assurance of His ever-present help.

*O God, our Good Shepherd, we praise
You and give thanks for Your protection.*

He'll Take Your Burden

Give your burdens to the Lord. He will carry them.
He will not permit the godly to slip or fall.
PSALM 55:22 TLB

David grieved the loss of a friendship to treachery. They had shared a close fellowship and worshipped the Lord together. Now David needed protection from someone he had trusted.

The burden of the betrayal was too heavy for David to carry alone. Because of the deceit, he had to be careful where he walked. His newly revealed enemy might come against him with more than smooth talking. David prayed to God for protection from the disloyal man, as well as for swift judgment. This false friend had violated his covenant with the Lord's anointed king.

Most of us have experienced the shock and grief of discovering a two-faced friend's betrayal. First we deny it. It can't be true. Then anger steeps in our veins. Sadness or depression follows, until we finally accept that someone we cared about was capable of stabbing us in the back.

This burden is too heavy for us to bear, but not for the Lord. He lifts it with ease, as though a feather, and protects us from falling deeper into the unfaithful person's snare.

Heavenly Father, thank You for carrying our
burdens for us. Protect us from enemies
who masquerade as friends.

Stand Firm

Be gracious to me, O God, be gracious to me, for my
soul takes refuge in You; and in the shadow of Your
wings I will take refuge until destruction passes by.
PSALM 57:1 NASB

After Saul halted his pursuit of David to fight a raiding band of Philistines, a messenger reported seeing David in the wilderness of Engedi. Saul took an army of three thousand men to find him.

David and his six hundred soldiers hid in a cave. Imagine his trepidation when the king and his military force came to the entrance of his hideaway. He prayed for God's protection. The Lord answered with an added bonus—an opportunity to prove to Saul that he had no reason to fear or hate David. As the king entered the cave for personal business, David cut off a section of Saul's robe. He refused his men's prodding to kill the king. Saul was still the anointed of the Lord. When David confronted him with the portion of the robe, King Saul responded with repentance.

When God answers our prayers with an opportunity like David's, we must not bend to the prodding of temptation but stand firm in the Lord's integrity.

Gracious Lord, as we take refuge in the shadow
of Your wings, let us remember David's
uprightness and honor You in the same way.

Rescue Mission

*For He rescued us from the domain of darkness, and
transferred us to the kingdom of His beloved Son,
in whom we have redemption, the forgiveness of sins.*
COLOSSIANS 1:13–14 NASB

We were born with a death penalty hanging over our
heads. Adam's rebellious gene has been passed down
through the generations from Eden. But through
God's immeasurable love for us, He didn't merely
commute our sentence to life in prison; He granted
an absolute reprieve. We now have everlasting life in
freedom. The Lord obtained our release through the
sacrifice of His beloved Son, Jesus Christ, the only
physical manifestation of Himself.

When our circumstances bring us low, we can
find joy in the good news of Jesus Christ. Our belief
in Him means this mortal life will be the only hell
we will experience. Without Him, this life would be
the only heaven we would know. There is no better
rescue mission than being saved from the darkness
of Satan's clutches and delivered into the eternal
kingdom of Christ.

*O precious Father God, You alone have rescued us
from the domain of darkness through Christ Jesus.
We now have the assurance that You are with us even
now and will protect us from our earthly adversaries.*

His Protective Hand

The Lord will rescue me from every evil work and will bring me safely into His heavenly kingdom. To Him be the glory forever and ever! Amen.

2 TIMOTHY 4:18 HCSB

Paul, suffering under the persecution of Nero, knew his execution was imminent. Yet in his cold, damp dungeon, he continued to praise God. He requested from Timothy only his cloak for warmth and his books and parchments to carry on his teaching about Christ.

God called Paul to His ministry in an extraordinary summons. He allowed Paul to endure hardship, abuse, and illness but preserved his earthly life long enough to further the spread of the Gospel of Jesus Christ.

As I look back on my own life, God's protective hand is evident. He stayed with me through illness, injury, betrayal, the death of loved ones, and poverty. He allowed me to suffer these seemingly impossible life events to bring me closer to Him. I learned to trust Him, as I had to rely on His provision to meet my every need. Now and in the future, I will put my faith and trust in Him, as we all can.

Dear Lord, we trust in Your ultimate and final rescue from the evils of this world. You'll bring us safely home to be with You at Your appointed time.

A Pure Heart

Create in me a pure heart, O God,
and renew a steadfast spirit within me.
PSALM 51:10 NIV

King David crumbled under the shame of Nathan's indictment. David had sinned against the Lord through adultery (with Bathsheba), deceit (in lying to her husband, Uriah), and murder (in sending Uriah to be killed in battle). He succeeded in hiding his crimes from the public, but God knew what he'd done.

In sincere repentance, David pleaded with God to forgive him and to cleanse him of his unworthiness. Although the consequences of David's actions were destined to play out, God forgave him. He blessed him with a living son through his new wife, Bathsheba. That son, Solomon, would inherit the throne and build the temple.

Asking the Lord to create a pure heart within us is one prayer He will always answer in the affirmative. In this request, we humble ourselves before Him, set aside our selfish pride, and ask for His forgiveness for any of our sins. He will transform our hearts and renew an unwavering spirit within us in that moment.

Be gracious to us, O God, according to Your
loving-kindness. Create in us pure hearts and
forgive our transgressions against You.

Future Blessings

Then he told me what the vision meant:
"These bones," he said, "represent all the people of
Israel. They say: 'We have become a heap of
dried-out bones—all hope is gone.' "
 EZEKIEL 37:11 TLB

In Ezekiel's vision of the valley of scattered dry bones, God explained that they represented the whole house of Israel. Their hope had perished when the Babylonians took them captive as God's judgment for Israel's sin against Him. Even so, according to His covenant with the Israelites, God had a restoration plan ready to bless them in the future.

Sometimes a devastating tragedy appears hopeless. We wearily try to make sense of the situation but see only dried-up, lifeless bones. Where do we begin to put our disconnected life back together? The first step is to pray, then trust in God, then watch and wait.

God has a solution for us. Regardless of the cause of our tragic event, He has future blessings in store for us. Only the Lord has the power to bring us back to a life filled with the abundance of His everlasting love.

Dear God, You have the supreme ability to put Your
Spirit into dried bones to make them breathing human
beings again. We trust in You to transform our despair
into hope. We hear the Word of the Lord.

Cold Stone to Warm Flesh

*"And this is just what I did in Jerusalem; not only did I
lock up many of the saints in prisons, having received
authority from the chief priests, but also when they
were being put to death I cast my vote against them."*
ACTS 26:10 NASB

Paul stood in chains before King Agrippa to defend
himself against the charges. His own people had falsely
accused him of causing dissension in the synagogue.
As part of his statement to the king, Paul confessed
the evil acts he had zealously committed against the
members of the Way. He then testified about his
life-transforming meeting with Jesus on the road to
Damascus.

Memories of our past deeds haunt our hearts and
minds. We chastise ourselves for the unsavory acts we
committed before accepting the Lord's salvation. The
key word is *before*. We didn't have the Holy Spirit to
hold us accountable for our behavior until we believed
in Jesus Christ.

Paul persecuted and murdered Christians before he
met Jesus on the road to Damascus. God forgave him;
then He transformed his heart from cold stone to warm
flesh so he could evangelize many nations.

A leopard can't change its spots, but God will
change us if we let Him.

*Precious Lord, let the peace of
Christ rule in our transformed hearts.*

Continual Process

And do not be conformed to this world,
but be transformed by the renewing of your mind,
that you may prove what is that good and
acceptable and perfect will of God.
ROMANS 12:2 NKJV

"When in Rome, do as the Romans do." This statement is attributed to Ambrose, the archbishop of Milan in the fourth century. Augustine and his mother, Monica, had asked him about the difference in Christian fast days in Rome and Milan. Today, it means follow the culture and blend in with the people—the exact opposite of what Paul admonished the church in Rome three hundred years earlier.

Our inclination is to keep in step with those around us. We learn early in our childhood that being "different" brings ridicule from our peers. But Christ wants us to be distinct, to stand out from the pagan culture. We often hear people say, "She claims to be a Christian, but. . ." Our transformation isn't an instantaneous change; it's a continual process from the inside out. We struggle every day to walk in His light, but the Lord is with us every step of the way.

Heavenly Father, help us remain steadfast
in this wonderful transformation that is
taking place within our hearts.

God's Righteous Throne

For You have maintained my just cause; You have
sat on the throne judging righteously. You have
rebuked the nations, You have destroyed the wicked;
You have blotted out their name forever and ever.

PSALM 9:4–5 NASB

David always thanked the Lord. He praised Him for His
protection when in danger, for His forgiveness when
he sinned, and for avenging him against his wicked
enemies. When an opportunity arose for David to take
revenge on his own terms, he wisely declined and left
revenge to the Lord.

David called on God to destroy the wicked, not for
his own benefit, but for the deliverance of his people.
The pagan nations had to be judged for their corrupt
influence on and merciless oppression of the Israelites.

Do we desire to take revenge against the wicked
enemies who oppress our people? Some live inside
our borders, while others dwell on foreign soil. But
they have one goal in mind: to destroy this nation
that God built for His purpose. He called ordinary
men and women and gave them extraordinary wisdom
and strength to accomplish this great feat. As our
enemies revolt against us, let God judge them from
His righteous throne.

Almighty God, You have maintained our just cause.
We praise You for protecting us and for avenging
the wickedness our enemies have imposed on us.

Kindness for Evil

Repay no one evil for evil. Have regard for good things in the sight of all men. If it is possible, as much as depends on you, live peaceably with all men. Beloved, do not avenge yourselves, but rather give place to wrath; for it is written, "Vengeance is Mine, I will repay," says the Lord.
ROMANS 12:17–19 NKJV

Paul had more reasons than most people to desire vengeance. He suffered beatings, stoning, slander, and false arrests, yet he instructed his fellow Christians not to repay evil for evil. The abuse and persecutions he endured taught him to lean wholly on the Lord for everything—even revenge.

Our adversary, Satan, wants us to seek personal revenge on those who have wronged us. What better way to show the world that we don't trust our Lord than to take matters into our own hands? If God wants to use us in His plan to judge the wicked, we won't know unless we ask Him. And we can be certain that He will never ask us to sin against Him in any way. Repaying evil with kindness disrupts the enemy's plans. That's far better than revenge.

Father in heaven, we know that a vengeful heart robs us of our peace. We have learned to trust You for everything—even vengeance.

Wait Patiently

Rest in the LORD, and wait patiently for Him;
do not fret because of him who prospers
in his way, because of the man who
brings wicked schemes to pass.
PSALM 37:7 NKJV

Scam artists slink through neighborhoods with their smooth sales pitches for less-than-adequate security systems, not-so-handy handyman chores, or high-priced tools. It may look as if they get away with their plans. They think so, for a time. But be patient. God knows who they are and what they're doing.

David warned his people about men prospering in their wicked schemes. In his day, their plans were probably closer to taking over a kingdom than hocking faulty equipment. But David said not to fret about their prosperous evildoing. They and their fortunes will wither like the grass.

How is it possible not to fret? The money we lost in a scam could've gone toward a mortgage payment or purchased groceries or medicine. But God says to wait patiently for Him to act. He wants us to step back, stop worrying, and trust in Him. Be patient.

O Lord our God, calm our fretful thoughts with
Your peace as we wait patiently for You to
judge the wicked and their schemes.

Magnificent Miracle

Martha then said to Jesus, "Lord, if You had been here, my brother would not have died. Even now I know that whatever You ask of God, God will give You."
JOHN 11:21–22 NASB

Mary and Martha sent word to Jesus when their brother became seriously ill, expecting Him to rush to their side and heal Lazarus. They waited and waited, but Jesus didn't arrive in time. Their brother died.

Jesus loved Lazarus and his two sisters. When He received their message that Lazarus was sick, he remarked that the sickness would not end in death but show God's glory. He delayed two more days before returning to Bethany. God's timing was critical for His intentions. Lazarus had to be dead and entombed for at least four days so Jesus could more fully demonstrate the miracle of restoring Lazarus to life.

Deep in her grief, Martha held on to her faith in the Lord. While patiently waiting, she knew that even if Lazarus died, God would grant Jesus anything He asked.

The sisters had expected a small miracle, but God displayed His glory in a more magnificent phenomenon—He raised Lazarus from the dead.

*Lord, while we wait patiently for You to act,
let us keep in mind these two prominent and
remarkable points: Your timing and Your greatness.*

Unexpected Blessings

We should help others do what is right and build them up in the Lord. For even Christ didn't live to please himself. As the Scriptures say, "The insults of those who insult you, O God, have fallen on me." Such things were written in the Scriptures long ago to teach us. And the Scriptures give us hope and encouragement as we wait patiently for God's promises to be fulfilled.
ROMANS 15:2–4 NLT

God brings us to a certain point in our struggle, and then everything stops. We wonder when the other shoe will drop. What will happen next? How will He resolve the continuing issue?

We wait and wait and wait. . . .

Instead of pacing or chewing our fingernails, why not assist our loved ones with their needs? They might be pondering an important decision. We can counsel them in the Word and do our utmost to lead them in the right direction. While offering our help to others, the Lord might reveal to us His solution to our own dilemma. He moves in mysterious ways.

Our patience in waiting for the Lord will also prove to others that we trust Him, and it could result in unexpected blessings for our loved ones and us.

God, our Father, grant us wisdom through Your Word when we help others while waiting for You.

With Kindness and Understanding

The Lord's bond-servant must not be quarrelsome,
but be kind to all, able to teach, patient when
wronged, with gentleness correcting those who
are in opposition, if perhaps God may grant them
repentance leading to the knowledge of the truth.
2 Timothy 2:24–25 NASB

Paul gave Timothy a list of attributes a soldier of Christ should possess: strength in grace, discipline, dedication, diligence, honesty, gentleness, serenity, and patience. Of all the qualities he expects us to have, patience is the key. None of the others is possible without it.

Occasions will arise when it's necessary to correct new believers in our fellowship who oppose the truth of the Bible. They might be argumentative and frustrating, trying our patience with every unfounded contention they can imagine. Paul urges us to be gentle and unwearied for curative purposes. Since the opposite of patience is aggravation or intolerance, we can't persuade anyone with an irritated approach. That will only chase that person away from the Gospel. With kindness and understanding, we can lead him or her away from the darkness of false teaching and into the light of God's truth. God will supply the patience we need.

Gracious and loving God, may we speak the truth
in love to those young in their faith
and understanding of Your Word.

When Circumstances Go Awry

Refrain from anger and turn from wrath;
do not fret—it leads only to evil.
PSALM 37:8 NIV

Anger is one of the most flexible and powerful emotions we experience. It can range from mild annoyance to full-blown, seething, white-hot fury.

David was no stranger to anger. Nabal insulted David and his men with his refusal to share food after David's men had protected Nabal's herds and flocks in Carmel. This wasn't a mere slight to David, but a major affront. David's knee-jerk reaction resulted in his army of four hundred men girding their swords with the intent of killing Nabal and all his men. God sent Nabal's wife, Abigail, to avert the bloodshed. David's anger and fretting would have led to evil if not for God's intervention through Abigail.

What causes us to react in anger to our circumstances? A misunderstanding? Betrayal? Malfunctioning tools? Injustice? Politicians? Our outrage to these, and more, will blind us to how God wants us to respond to the offense. Sometimes it might seem impossible to control our tempers when circumstances go awry. But let us remember David's escape from calamity through Abigail's kindness and allow God to keep us from spiteful actions.

O God in heaven, calm our hearts and minds
as we struggle against our anger.

Solomon's Wise Advice

He who is slow to anger is better than the mighty,
and he who rules his spirit, than he
who captures a city.
PROVERBS 16:32 NASB

I claim to have a slow-burning fuse, but woe to the person who lights it! There have been occasions when someone, either unwittingly or by design, snipped a yard or two from my fuse.

It takes more strength than I can muster to control my temper in a spontaneous confrontation. If I expect the altercation, through a growing animosity or warning from a friend, then I can prepare for it in my prayer time. God will give me the calmness of spirit and the words I need to deflect the hostile dispute. But I must pray before the incident. When my enemies catch me unawares and spring their verbal attacks on me, there is no time to step aside and pray.

Solomon's advice in this proverb shows us that the time to pray for temper control or to decelerate our anger isn't right before an incident. Daily prayer will keep us in God's protective arms, and He will grant us the power to restrain our anger.

Almighty God, thank You for Solomon's
wisdom on how to contain our anger.

Let Anger Go

Be angry and do not sin. Don't let the sun go down on your anger, and don't give the Devil an opportunity.
EPHESIANS 4:26–27 HCSB

Is it possible for us to be angry and not sin? Isn't all our anger steeped in selfish pride?

In righteous anger, God evicted Adam and Eve from Eden. They tainted the perfect world He created.

God's righteous anger burned against the Israelites for turning away from Him and worshipping false gods. They sacrificed their babies to the idols Molech and Baal.

In righteous anger, Jesus drove the money changers out of the temple. They turned His house of worship into an impious marketplace.

Our culture calls good evil and evil good, and it proclaims that sin doesn't exist, distorting God's Word. Sharing in God's anger at these deceptions is not sinful, but Paul warns us that it has a time limit. At dusk, the oncoming of darkness, we let go of the anger. Clutching it, instead of praying for the souls of the wicked, is prideful sin. That opens the door for Satan to tempt us.

Righteous Father God, we share Your wrath when evil people profane Your holiness. Help us release our anger to You.

God's Wardrobe

Let all bitterness and wrath and anger and clamor and slander be put away from you, along with all malice. Be kind to one another, tender-hearted, forgiving each other, just as God in Christ also has forgiven you.

EPHESIANS 4:31–32 NASB

Put away bitterness, wrath, anger, clamor, slander, and malice? Is that possible in today's culture? Satan wants us to continue wearing the nasty rags we inherited from him before we accepted Christ's gift of eternal life. Now that our souls are out of his reach, he promotes the "old self" attire in his efforts to neutralize us. Bitterness rots our hearts from the inside out. Wrath, anger, clamor, slander, and malice hurt those near us and steal our souls' peace.

It is possible to throw off these tattered garments and don the pristine gowns God provides. We replace bitterness with kindness. Wrath and its entourage cannot exist in the presence of Christ's tenderhearted forgiveness. Paul's words are sewn into the seams of our unsullied wardrobes. As we dress ourselves in the scriptures, we neutralize our wicked adversary.

Gracious and loving Lord, You have renewed our minds, adorning us with Your Spirit. Remind us through Your Word to be kind to one another.

Supreme Justice

God will turn the sins of evil people back on them.
He will destroy them for their sins. The LORD
our God will destroy them.
PSALM 94:23 NLT

David brought his charges against the wicked to the Lord, asking for justice. They haughtily boasted of their murderous cruelty, believing God didn't see the oppression they inflicted on others. Then they scoffed at David when he tried to warn them of God's coming judgment. They didn't recognize their own foolish self-aggrandizement.

We wonder why God allows evil people to pervert the laws to meet their own arrogant needs. They band together, apparently unhindered, to destroy the righteous. They've been with us since Adam took his first bite of the forbidden fruit. It seems impossible to stop them, but the Lord has let it be known: God is not mocked. He who created eyes sees all their deeds and will judge. What they have sown will sprout up against them as prickly thorns and thistles. God said He will turn the evil acts back on the wicked, and His justice is supreme.

Almighty God, we trust Your absolute justice as You pronounce Your verdict on the impenitent evildoers.

Doing Good

Better a little with righteousness
than much gain with injustice.

PROVERBS 16:8 NIV

When facing impossible challenges that life presents, we have an advantage over unbelievers. We can see God's perspective. He wants us to enjoy the blessings and rewards of diligent work. Not that a windfall is bad, if it comes from a righteous source. I call the acts of bending rules or breaking laws blessing thieves.

I once worked with a woman who gained salary increases through illicit temptations to her boss. Her paycheck thrived, but her actions killed the trust and respect of her coworkers, for both her and the boss.

Robbers might enjoy their plunder for a short while, before they are caught and sent to prison.

A friend of my husband's confessed to a past life of gambling. He said he held up his thousands of dollars of winnings and proclaimed, "This is my God!" The next day, he was broke and in jail, with a contrite heart.

Satan wants us to believe that injustices like cheating or stealing are better providers than honesty. But our justice is in the eternal reward of doing good in the sight of the Lord.

O Father God, we desire to live
righteously in Your eyes in all we do.

God's Justice

Woe to those who call evil good and good evil,
who substitute darkness for light and light
for darkness, who substitute bitter
for sweet and sweet for bitter.

Isaiah 5:20 HCSB

In this "Woe to. . ." chapter, Isaiah pronounced God's denunciation of Judah. Their blatant sin of avarice led to pagan alliances, which led to idolatry, which led to abandoning their trust in the Lord. He had set them apart as His precious vineyard, but they produced only worthless fruit. God's justice required that Assyria and Babylon punish them for their rejection of His commandments.

Unbelievers in our culture today malign Christians and accuse us of intolerance because we believe in the truth of the Bible. They call it evil. They want to extinguish our light because it exposes their covetousness, alliance with God's adversaries, and self-worship.

How do we fight this impossible battle? We pray God will issue the same indictments against Christ's enemies as He did against the worthless vineyard. Woe to them when the Lord answers our pleas for His justice, for it will come swift, heavy, and without mercy.

O Lord, You are a just God, righteous in every way.
We pray for Your judgment on those
who are against You.

Continued Daily Prayers

*Then these men said, "We shall not find any charge
against this Daniel unless we find it against
him concerning the law of his God."*

DANIEL 6:5 NKJV

The commissioners and satraps sought to discredit Daniel. King Darius planned to appoint him as one of three top commissioners over the kingdom. Daniel would surely expose their graft to the king. They found no hint of corruption in Daniel though. The only case they could build against him was his faithfulness to God.

King Darius signed their religious injunction, declaring it illegal to pray to anyone except the king. But Daniel remained loyal to the Lord. Instead of panicking when he learned of the edict, he continued his daily prayers. Daniel willingly broke man's law to uphold God's.

These government officials singled out Daniel because of his religious beliefs. God acquitted him through the lions' closed mouths. Then God used King Darius to execute His justice against those who maliciously accused Daniel. God opened the lions' mouths to devour those evildoers.

Let us look to Daniel's case when we see persecution and seek justice. God allowed the king's evil men to be thrown into the trap they designed for Daniel.

*Great is Your faithfulness, O God our Father!
Close the mouths of our accusers, we pray.*

Righteous Judge

Therefore the law is ignored and justice is never upheld. For the wicked surround the righteous; therefore justice comes out perverted.

HABAKKUK 1:4 NASB

The prophet Habakkuk questioned God about the unbridled wickedness in Judah. Where was justice? Had the Lord forgotten them?

God replied with His clear guilty verdict on them. He planned to send the Chaldeans to invade Judah and capture her people. The Chaldeans were exceedingly cruel and more evil than the nation of Judah. God, in His sovereignty, will allow even the vile deeds of men to carry out His purposes.

The Lord had waited patiently for His people to return to Him. Instead, they inched farther away. He was prepared to perform the duties of prosecutor, defense counsel, and judge.

Our misused justice system makes us think God has forgotten us. It seems impossible to correct the unfair bias we observe. We might ask God: Where is our justice? Judges, attorneys, and legislators all function in finite human standards. But the Lord is omniscient and clearly sees all the evidence of the wicked. He alone has the ability and power to judge righteously.

Holy God, we pray for Your mercy on us as You execute justice on our enemies.

His Plans and Purposes

The LORD will perfect that which concerns me;
Your mercy, O LORD, endures forever;
do not forsake the works of Your hands.
PSALM 138:8 NKJV

David continually praised God for His bountiful mercy. God answered David's prayers in impossible circumstances and showed David where he fit into His plans.

How often do we remember to praise the Lord during our impossible situations? In our darkest, saddest, or most tempestuous moments, it could always be worse. We wring our hands and ask, "How could it possibly be worse?" Facing the fretful malady completely alone—without the Lord—that would make it worse. We might be surrounded by friends and loved ones at any given moment, but they will each step back, turn, and leave. They have their own life issues that need attention. The Lord will never leave His children. He is strong enough, big enough, and merciful enough to stand by each of us with His open arms waiting to embrace us.

In His everlasting mercy and loving-kindness, He will accomplish what concerns us according to His plans and purposes.

Loving Father, we give thanks to You with our whole
heart for standing by us and embracing us
with Your grace, mercy, and love.

Great Love

But God, being rich in mercy, because of His great love with which He loved us, even when we were dead in our transgressions, made us alive together with Christ (by grace you have been saved).

Ephesians 2:4–5 nasb

We were spiritually dead in our sins, *but God* in His mercy made us alive again through Jesus Christ, our Savior. We walked in darkness as children of wrath, *but God* in His mercy gave us the Light of the World. We indulged in the desires of the flesh, *but God* in His mercy gave us the desires of His heart.

When our impossible circumstances drag us to the brink of hopelessness, we can hold on to "but God." Being rich in mercy means He has an everlasting well that will never run dry. In His mercy, God forgave and restored the Israelites. He forgave Peter for betraying Jesus and Saul of Tarsus for persecuting the early Christians. In His mercy, He will carry us through any loss, tragedy, or disaster. God's mercy endures forever.

God loved us before He created us. In His mercy, he showers us with His redeeming love.

Merciful Father, thank You for Your great love with which You have loved us. Thank You for Your endless supply of loving-kindness.

Holy Spirit

Watch over your heart with all diligence,
for from it flow the springs of life.
PROVERBS 4:23 NASB

In scripture, the heart is considered the core of our being. It's more than an organ that pumps blood throughout the body; it's the inner nature of our minds or souls. King Solomon instructs us to guard our hearts like a sentry to impede intruders. The enemy will try every deception to gain access into our inner being. He wants to plant thorns of malice in the fertile soil of our minds and to water them with his embittered hatred.

What is in our hearts determines our actions and reactions. Jesus said if we carry hatred for fellow human beings, then we have murdered them in our hearts. So, what do we harbor inside us—evil thoughts or goodness? Do springs of life flow through us, or do we find a dried-up dust bowl?

When images of those who have hurt me in the past come to mind and lead to anger, I know the thoughts are not from God. He wants me to enjoy His peace. My inner Sentry, the Holy Spirit, reminds me to pray for those people and praise God for His everlasting love.

Loving Father, help us set up Your Sentry to guard our
hearts and thoughts from Satan's seeds of bitterness.

Read, Study, Pray

Watch yourselves so you don't lose what we have worked for, but that you may receive a full reward.

2 John 8 HCSB

In this letter, John first praised the "chosen lady" (v. 1 NLV) for evidence that her children were walking in God's truth and expressing His love to those around them.

He then warned her about deceptive teaching slipping into the church. Some men tried to mislead the members with their own unbelief in the incarnation of God in Christ Jesus. John advised them not to have any fellowship with, or even acknowledge, these individuals. An excellent word of caution, for a rotten apple quickly spreads its decay through the barrel.

We often weary ourselves arguing with misguided men and women about God's truth. They use Bible verses out of context or extrabiblical writings to spread their rotten apples. To those who are weak in faith, these deceivers sound convincing. The best way we can discern and affirm God's true message is to read and study His Word and pray every day. Then we will enjoy the blessings of His abiding grace, mercy, and peace.

Gracious God, we trust in You and Your holy Word to help us guard against persuasive false teachers.

Pray Confidently

O love the LORD, all ye his saints: for the LORD
preserveth the faithful, and plentifully rewardeth
the proud doer. Be of good courage, and he shall
strengthen your heart, all ye that hope in the LORD.
PSALM 31:23–24 KJV

David prayed for the Lord to deliver him from his enemies; he then glorified God for answering the prayer. God had silenced the opposing forces and relieved David's distress. Speaking from experience as he affirmed God's faithfulness, David inspired the people to love the Lord and take courage in Him. He proclaimed his trust and total reliance on God to protect them.

We don't have enough fingers and toes to count how many times God has answered our prayers to rescue and protect us. He wants us to come to Him confidently when we are in distress or danger, even with our minor annoyances. Knowing that He holds us in His loving hands gives us strength of heart to scrape our way through the difficulty. Then we can show our love for the Lord, like David did, in praising Him each time He answers our prayers and delivers us from our enemies.

O Lord our God, we love You and put our trust
in You to strengthen us and give us courage.

Courage and Confidence

*"And now, Lord, take note of their threats,
and grant that Your bond-servants may
speak Your word with all confidence."*

ACTS 4:29 NASB

When Peter and John had been released from jail, they went to their fellow apostles to report the rulers' latest order. It forbade them from further preaching the Gospel.

These devout men didn't cave to the rulers' commands and give up. They immediately raised their unified petition to God. In their prayer, they didn't ask the Lord to condemn their enemies. They didn't ask Him to deliver them from their plight and transport them into a new ministry. They praised Him and asked only for the courage to continue in the work the Lord had given them to accomplish.

God knows the threats that His enemies make against us. He is fully aware of the snares and hardships wicked people want to inflict on us. He also knows, as we do, that He is greater than any opponent the evil one puts forward to impede our efforts. In that truth, let us petition God for His courage and confidence when enemies of the faith oppose us.

*Lord God in heaven, take note of our enemies'
bullying and grant us confidence to continue
to proclaim the good news of Jesus Christ.*

Be Alert

Keep your eyes open for spiritual danger;
stand true to the Lord; act like men; be strong;
and whatever you do, do it with kindness.
1 CORINTHIANS 16:13–14 TLB

In the middle of closing his letter to the Corinthians, Paul plopped in the statement to keep their eyes open for, or be alert to, spiritual danger. He had mentioned Apollos and the delay of his visit and then told the Corinthians that they should subject themselves to the first members who were wholly devoted to Christ in Achaia, Stephanas and his family. The warning to be watchful might seem out of place, being unrelated to the general information for the church. But Paul put it there for a reason.

He charged the believers in Corinth to stay true to the teachings of the Lord because some were spreading a counterfeit doctrine. They were teaching that the resurrection of Jesus Christ was a hoax. Paul wanted his fellow believers to courageously confront these deceivers, in kindness, before their lies seeped into the church.

Even in our casual conversations or correspondence to each other, we must always be alert to the dangers of false teachings. We may plop those warnings in when they are needed.

Dear God, our Father, we heed the warnings
of Your faithful servant Paul and seek Your
courage to confront deceitful teachers.

Courage to Overcome

We use God's mighty weapons, not worldly weapons, to knock down the strongholds of human reasoning and to destroy false arguments.

2 CORINTHIANS 10:4 NLT

Some of Paul's opponents challenged his reputation as a strong leader for the church. Because of his meek and gentle manner, they called him a coward. A coward? This courageous man was ostracized, beaten, stoned, and imprisoned for boldly proclaiming the salvation of the Lord Jesus Christ. His actions speak more of bravery than cowardice.

Paul was reluctant to boast of himself, but for the sake of his ministry, he had to defend his authority as an apostle of Jesus Christ. Rather than take to the sword or resort to slanderous language, he confronted his hecklers with the Word of God. Christ Himself had trained Paul and given him authority to oversee the church. If necessary, he could call on the Lord to sternly discipline them.

How do we respond when opponents of Christ malign our reputations as born-again believers? They call us hypocrites because we still struggle with the sin nature we inherited from Adam. Using God's weapons of meekness and gentleness, along with His mighty Word, we will have the courage to overcome and destroy their false arguments.

Almighty God, we take courage through Your Word to defend our Christian faith against those who oppose You.

Discouragement to Encouragement

*And because of my imprisonment, many of the
Christians here seem to have lost their fear of chains!
Somehow my patience has encouraged them,
and they have become more and more
bold in telling others about Christ.*

PHILIPPIANS 1:14 TLB

The members of the church in Philippi erroneously presumed that Paul's incarceration prevented him from preaching the Gospel. But he proved them wrong. Paul used the chain that bound him to a soldier to spread the Gospel throughout the whole praetorian guard. His enthusiasm for the Lord must have been contagious, because courage to teach about Jesus Christ grew dramatically in other Christians. Fully aware that it might lead to their imprisonment, they still did not yield to intimidation.

Our discouraging circumstances can be flipped over to encourage us instead. We can turn our predicament into a podium, as Paul did, and as these believers did. . . A young man serving a prison sentence used his time to study the Bible and effectively teach the Gospel to other inmates. A widow had her late husband's Bible at his funeral for visitors to sign next to a favorite verse. Curious unbelievers searched through it as well, and some of them inquired about Jesus.

*O Lord our God, we pray for the courage to use our
"chains" to spread Your good news about Jesus Christ.*

In Plenty or in Want

*Keep deception and lies far from me, give me neither
poverty nor riches; feed me with the food that is my
portion, that I not be full and deny You and say,
"Who is the LORD?" Or that I not be in want and
steal, and profane the name of my God.*

PROVERBS 30:8–9 NASB

Discontentment began with Satan. Spending eternity
with God as an angel wasn't enough for him. He defied
the Lord and stole a third of the heavenly host with
him. Then he seduced Eve in her gullible state. The
fruit of the other trees no longer satisfied her.

God provided atonement for humans through the
blood of Jesus Christ, but not for the angels. Satan
has since targeted us with his weapons of misery and
dissatisfaction.

Our circumstances are like balancing scales. A
little neediness keeps us humble. Too much neediness
tempts us to covet and steal. Great wealth might
cause us to be haughty or make it possible for us to
graciously help those less fortunate.

What is the median weight for our scales? In plenty
and in want, we thank God. He provides all we need if
we set aside our worries and ask Him. God will dispel
Satan's misery and dissatisfaction.

*Gracious God, our contentment lies in the
assurance of spending eternity with You.
The tree of life is good enough for us.*

Positive Perspective

"Vanity of vanities," says the Preacher, "All is vanity."
ECCLESIASTES 12:8 NKJV

Solomon teaches three key principles of life: Human effort is futile, this mortal life is unpredictable, and death is certain. He reminds us of our own brevity and the reality of growing old. If we look no deeper into this lesson, we would sink into the quagmire of depression.

There is equity in the good and unpleasant events in our lives. A new job, filled with hope for the future, doesn't work out. It seems devastating until God reveals His plans for a better opportunity. We struggle against an impossible situation to no avail. Then we pray about it. The dilemma is mysteriously resolved in an instant.

A positive perspective is the beginning of contentment. We recognize and take pleasure in what God has provided, trust in His control, and faithfully seek His kingdom and righteousness.

God teaches His three key principles of life: His efforts are wonderful, our mortal life is an adventure, and death is a door to eternity with Him.

O Lord, we will praise You and give thanks in all times, in our youth and old age, in our troubles and tranquility. For we live in the blessed contentment of You.

Trust for Today

"So do not worry about tomorrow; for tomorrow will care for itself. Each day has enough trouble of its own."
MATTHEW 6:34 NASB

Worry doesn't add a single day or even an hour to our life span. With all its trappings of gritting teeth, adrenalin rushes, heart flutters, and shortness of breath, there's a good chance it will actually shorten our lives. We tell our bodies to calm down, but do they listen? Mine doesn't. When we feel the onset of anxiety, sometimes a quick prayer will nip it in the bud.

Jesus points out that even birds are content to let God feed them. He created them with an internal trust-in-Him feature. Flowers never say, "I have nothing to wear." God cares about the well-being of His wildlife—and even more so about ours. Let us be content with each day, giving it a chance to generate new opportunities for us.

Living one day at a time doesn't mean we can shirk our responsibility to prepare for the future. Preparation today holds back tomorrow's troubles.

File yesterday in memories. Trust the Lord in this day, for we have no guarantees for tomorrow.

Our loving Father, every day You give us is a blessing. Let us be content and grateful to You for each one.

Message of Hope

Our hearts ache, but we always have joy. We are poor,
but we give spiritual riches to others. We own
nothing, and yet we have everything.
2 CORINTHIANS 6:10 NLT

While Paul experienced multiple hardships in his ministry, he encouraged the new Christians in Corinth with his example of humble contentment. He didn't consider riches in the material sense but in the eternality of his relationship with Christ. Spreading the Word of truth and grace, he shared God's spiritual wealth and brought much joy to any who believed.

We find contentment in recognizing the true value of God's riches, not the world's. Money and possessions don't last. All the *things* we care about today could be gone tomorrow. But nothing can take away our joy in the everlasting love of the Father, our intimate relationship with Jesus Christ, and the prudent guidance of the Holy Spirit. These eternal possessions are far greater than material wealth.

Like Paul, let us faithfully share God's kingdom and righteousness with the lost right now, for we live for the life to come.

O Lord, the God of our salvation, bless us with
Your joy so that we may find contentment in
sharing Your message of hope with others.

Steadfast God

It is better to take refuge in the
LORD than to trust in people.
PSALM 118:8 NLT

When we say we're in a tight spot, we're describing a time of distress. David said that when he called on the Lord, He answered and set David in a "large place" (Psalm 31:8 NLV). No longer bound by the "tight spot" of his enemies, David could move about freely. Each time David prayed, whether for protection, deliverance, or forgiveness, he knew he could trust God to answer his petition.

David trusted his father-in-law to treat him like family, but Saul continuously hunted him down to kill him. David trusted his first wife to be loyal, but she derided him when he brought God's ark into the city. The only person David could trust was the prophet Nathan, and he died.

We trust friends and loved ones, some with our confidences and some with our lives. They will be there for us when they can, but incidents, obligations, or other distractions will pull them away. People will disappoint us, but God is steadfast in His love for us. We can always trust Him to be with us, no matter what happens.

We give thanks to You, Lord,
for Your loving-kindness is everlasting.

Flourish

He who trusts in his riches will fall, but the
righteous will flourish like the green leaf.
PROVERBS 11:28 NASB

When God offered King Solomon anything he wanted, he didn't selfishly ask for long life or the death of his enemies or great wealth. He chose wisdom instead. He could best serve the Lord with an understanding heart that would help him discern between good and evil to judge righteously. God also blessed him with what he did not request—riches and honor. No king, before or after Solomon's reign, enjoyed such fame and fortune. The king trusted in God, not his great wealth, for all his needs.

The temptation to trust in material assets to save us is a powerful lure to overcome. But money really doesn't buy happiness, nor can it bribe death. It is a temporary gift in this mortal world.

Whether we're wealthy, poor, or in the middle, God is our Provider. The only riches we can count on to last forever are God's love, His mercy, and His gift of eternal life. Putting our trust in Him, we will flourish in His righteousness.

O God, our bountiful Father, everything belongs to
You. We trust in You for all our provisions.

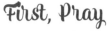

First, Pray

Indeed, we personally had a death sentence
within ourselves, so that we would not trust
in ourselves but in God who raises the dead.
2 Corinthians 1:9 HCSB

Paul and Timothy had suffered such affliction in Asia that Paul considered it important to share the burden with the Corinthian church members. He said they had "despaired even of life" (2 Corinthians 1:8 KJV). We don't know the cause of their distress. It could've been a serious illness or more violent assaults from Christ's enemies. Either way, they came dangerously close to death.

Most of us mentally run through all possible solutions for our challenging circumstances. Then we might search other resources to verify that the remedy we chose is correct. When everything else fails, all that's left for us to do is pray. Shouldn't prayer be our first step?

Paul reminds us that trusting in ourselves is futile. Although God gave us the intelligence to reason for ourselves and take action, we still need Him. Can we make blind men see, heal the sick, or raise the dead? Let us petition the One who can do all these miracles, and more, before relying on our feeble human efforts. We can trust Him with our lives.

Father of mercies, when we are beyond
our strength and despair even of life,
touch our hearts with Your love and healing.

Count on God's Word

Then the word of the LORD came to Jeremiah after the king had burned the scroll and the words which Baruch had written at the dictation of Jeremiah, saying, "Take again another scroll and write on it all the former words that were on the first scroll which Jehoiakim the king of Judah burned."

JEREMIAH 36:27–28 NASB

The Lord commanded Jeremiah to write concerning His coming judgment for Judah. If they heeded God's warning, they might abandon their wicked ways and be spared. The scribe Baruch wrote what Jeremiah dictated. But when the court officials read it to the king, Jehoiakim slashed the scroll and burned it.

God persevered. He commanded Jeremiah and Baruch to rewrite the warning—and added more prophecies of judgment against the defiant king.

Throughout history, attempts have been made to destroy God's Word or prohibit its distribution, but God's Word prevails. A missionary in Ukraine handed out Bibles to thousands of teenagers in a field where decades earlier communist officials had burned all the Bibles in the region. My friend watched his Bible-filled suitcase pass through the X-ray machine in a Middle East airport. The security guard had his back to the screen, chatting with my friend.

We can always count on God's Word to be available in our difficult times.

Dear Lord, everything around us will crumble, but Your Word perseveres forever.

Persevere

*"And so I tell you, keep on asking, and you will receive
what you ask for. Keep on seeking, and you will find.
Keep on knocking, and the door will be opened to you."*

LUKE 11:9 NLT

Persistent prayer doesn't entail uttering chants without giving thought to our petition. Jesus teaches us to persevere in our heartfelt prayers. Because we know the Son, we have confidence that the Father will hear and answer.

The continual knocking at heaven's door doesn't move the Lord to respond to us. He knows our needs before we ask. We persevere to strengthen our faith. Do we come to Him in doubt or hope? We think our needs are too small, too big, or too peculiar for God to consider them. Or do we deem ourselves unworthy of His attention?

Jesus noted that an earthly father wouldn't substitute a snake for a fish or a scorpion for an egg when responding to his child's request. We have no reason to question our heavenly Father's intentions. If we seek Him with all our heart, we will find Him.

God loves and values us. Let us persevere in our prayers and thanksgivings, waiting expectantly for God to open His door to us.

*Abba Father, we come to You with a heart of
gratitude and hope, confident that You
hear and answer our prayers.*

Faithful in Troubles

Indeed we count them blessed who endure.
You have heard of the perseverance of Job and
seen the end intended by the Lord—that the
Lord is very compassionate and merciful.
JAMES 5:11 NKJV

James used Job's example to encourage the recipients of his letter. In all his afflictions, Job persevered in his moral integrity. He raised the bar for the rest of us in faithfulness and endurance.

As we face our hardships, we might be tempted to fib, cheat, or steal to wheedle some relief from our suffering. We might think that no one is watching, but there is One who sees everything we do. God knows what dwells in our hearts and minds.

Our behavior can reflect our steadfast devotion to the Lord. We can encourage other Christians to stay true to the course or draw unbelievers into the family of God when we say no to temptation. We are often unaware of the examples we set for others.

Let us persevere in our moral integrity while enduring every hardship—and also while enjoying God's merciful blessings.

Merciful God, we pray for Your strength to
help us persevere in our faithfulness to
You in all our afflictions.

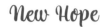

New Hope

So be truly glad! There is wonderful joy ahead, even though the going is rough for a while down here.

1 PETER 1:6 TLB

The night is darkest just before dawn. A pale light appears on the horizon and grows brighter by the minute. Then birds sing, squirrels scamper, and flowers open their petals to the rising sun. A new day brings new hope.

Peter wanted to prepare the Christians throughout the Roman Empire for Nero's coming persecutions. The pagans' hatred for them was escalating from mere annoyances to terrifying hostilities. He assured his new converts that their earthly trials would be short-lived compared to the imperishable joy that God had reserved for them. An everlasting inheritance awaited them in heaven.

The proof of our faith is evident as we persevere in joy knowing that our trials are temporary. We too have that same inheritance of God's eternal love, dispelling the darkness forever, when He calls us home.

The dawn's light of joy awaits us at the end of the dark tunnel of our suffering. Every new day provides new hope for us as we serve our mighty God.

O God, our Father, Your promise that our heavenly inheritance has been firmly fixed brings us joy and strengthens our faith as we persevere through our worldly troubles.

Of the Lord

But you belong to God, my dear children. You have already won a victory over those people, because the Spirit who lives in you is greater than the spirit who lives in the world.

1 JOHN 4:4 NLT

False teachers in John's day attempted to lead new Christians astray. He warned believers to be alert to these evil prophets who operated under the promptings of demonic spirits. He taught them not to trust every spirit, but to make sure they were of the Lord. The defining principle was the belief that God came in the flesh as Jesus Christ.

John walked with Jesus, witnessed His miracles and transfiguration, and watched Him die, rise again, and ascend to heaven. What more credible evidence could be found that affirmed Jesus Christ was the incarnation of God? Believers in John's day won their victory over false teachers through the indwelling of the Holy Spirit, which helped them discern the truth.

The enemies of God still make every effort to conceal, twist, or counterfeit His Word. We also must test every spirit to guard against misleading doctrine. We also win our victory over these falsehoods through the Holy Spirit, as well as the full evidence of the Bible.

Thank You, Father God, for guiding us, through the Holy Spirit, to protect Your Word.

Winning

*For whatever is born of God overcomes the world;
and this is the victory that has overcome
the world—our faith.*

1 JOHN 5:4 NASB

We are in constant battle with our sin nature. Our desires to obey and please God conflict with the lures of the fleshly world. Every day, we wearily struggle with decisions that either draw us closer to the Lord or push Him away a little bit.

The apostle John says that relying on the Holy Spirit to guide us lessens the burden to keep God's commandments. Our obedience leads to a deeper fellowship with our heavenly Father, as well as our family in Christ. This strong bond weakens our sin nature and gives us the spiritual strength to adhere to a life that delights God.

Our love for Jesus grows our faith, and our faith increases our love for Him in perpetuity. We show God's love in us when we support each other during weak moments and rejoice together in the Lord's blessings.

We will overcome the world, though it hates us, with our faith in our Lord and Savior, Jesus Christ.

*Beloved God, we praise You for our victory over
the world. Let us strive to please only You.*

Final Victory

"And He will wipe away every tear from their eyes;
and there will no longer be any death; there will
no longer be any mourning, or crying, or pain;
the first things have passed away."

REVELATION 21:4 NASB

God will make all things new. He will cause the first creation to pass away because of the effects of sin. The apostle Peter wrote, "The heavens will pass away with a roar and the elements will be destroyed with intense heat, and the earth and its works will be burned up" (2 Peter 3:10 NASB).

God's new heaven and new earth will be immune to Satan and his demons. They will be cast away, never to plague humankind with temptations again. It was sin that introduced tears, death, mourning, and pain. Those miseries cannot exist without sin.

Until that time, we will continue to endure sin's corruption in our mortal lives. But we'll have God by our side, with His arms around us to protect and guide us. He will provide for our needs, as He always has.

And we take solace in our hope of the final victory—over death!

Almighty God, we know and affirm that because we
believe in Jesus Christ, the risen Lord, we will be with
You in the new creation. Come, Lord Jesus.

A Lesson in Restoration

"I opened to my beloved, but my beloved had turned away and had gone! My heart went out to him as he spoke. I searched for him but I did not find him; I called him but he did not answer me."

SONG OF SOLOMON 5:6 NASB

In this chapter of Solomon's love poem, the wife cites her reasons for denying her husband entry to the home. It was late at night. She had undressed for bed. Her clean feet would get dirty. When she finally opened the door, he had gone. Their first spat. But they immediately reconciled.

My grandmother confided that she once considered leaving my grandfather. He was a scoundrel in his younger days. She was glad she didn't seek a divorce. The love they shared in their later years offset the grief of their early marriage.

Marital strife affects the entire family, in-laws included. Self-centered pride seems to be the number one culprit. If that issue can be resolved, the marriage could last a lifetime.

Divorce is unavoidable in some circumstances, such as abuse, violent criminal acts, or adultery. But if at all possible, consider Solomon's love poem for a lesson in restoration. "I am my beloved's and my beloved is mine" (Song of Solomon 6:3 NASB).

Loving Father, I pray for love to return to families in the throes of separation or divorce.

In God's Peace and Love

And if a house be divided against itself,
that house cannot stand.
MARK 3:25 KJV

To discredit Jesus, the scribes alleged that Beelzebul possessed His spirit when He cast out demons. The Jewish leaders used the name of the pagan idol to refer to Satan.

Jesus pointed out the absurdity of their allegation. Indeed, how could Satan cast himself out of himself? In His rebuttal to the scribes, Jesus held up a mirror to their hypocrisy. Was the doctrinal squabbling of the scribes fracturing their leadership? One issue united them: their hatred for Jesus Christ.

What divides families against themselves today? Sometimes parents fail to teach their children to respect others. An absence of parental guidance often leaves children vulnerable to evil influences. Many of us spend more time on our electronic devices than speaking to each other, existing under the same roof as a splintered family. Multiple schedules create an atmosphere of chaos and stress. The one dynamic that could reunite families is love for Jesus Christ.

In a home where parents and children set aside time for prayer and for reading and discussing the Bible together, they dwell in God's peace and love.

Heavenly Father, many families are in
distress. Please show us how to have undivided
households founded on Your peace and love.

Come to Him

Behold, children are a gift of the LORD,
the fruit of the womb is a reward.
PSALM 127:3 NASB

The signs that a child is on the way can bring joy to a woman who longs for motherhood.

But some women view a new pregnancy as a burden. There's no room in their future career for a child. An impoverished woman or a mother of an already large family doesn't have the means to feed another mouth. Parents coerce their unwed daughters into ending the new life growing inside them for the sake of family reputation.

What happened to our trust in the Lord? Maybe that God-planned child could have saved the woman from a disastrous career. Do we not realize that God will supply the needs of impoverished families? Could we not offer the unexpected baby for adoption to a childless couple?

Jesus said of all children, "The kingdom of God belongs to such as these" (Mark 10:14 NASB). God loves and values every zygote that is, was, and will be formed in the womb. He also loves women who have aborted His babies, and He will mend their devastated hearts, if only they will come to Him.

Help us, O Lord, to comfort Your daughters who
battle with the dreadful aftermath of abortion.

In His Peace

"These things I have spoken to you, so that in Me you may have peace. In the world you have tribulation, but take courage; I have overcome the world."

JOHN 16:33 NASB

Where does Jesus say we have peace? In Him. Where does He say we have tribulation? In the world.

Distress and suffering are a natural part of this sinful world, having been introduced through Adam. The whole world groans in pain. But Jesus said we have peace in Him.

God allows certain afflictions to strengthen us or keep us humble (think Paul's thorn in his side). Pride goes before the fall. But Jesus said we have peace in Him.

God chastises us with hardships when we disobey Him. As His children, we require discipline to keep our paths straight. But Jesus said we have peace in Him.

Jesus knew His disciples would scatter in fear at His arrest and trial. They would return in courage with God's help. He could still use them, giving them His peace in their tribulation.

Jesus has overcome the world and will return, in His time, as the triumphant, conquering King. Until that day, we will endure our worldly afflictions in His peace.

Lord God, we have hope during our most impossible tribulations because Jesus said we have peace in Him. He said it. We believe it.

Pursue His Peace

Turn away from evil and do what is good;
seek peace and pursue it.
PSALM 34:14 HCSB

David and his men showed respect and kindness to other shepherds at shearing time. He also helped guard their sheep in the wilderness. He sought peace with Saul despite Saul's attempts to kill him. He embraced Jonathan's son as though he were his own and gave all that had belonged to Saul to the boy.

Departing from evil can be difficult because we expect evil to be blatantly obvious. But it can be as obscure as a misspoken word. As we inadvertently stir the pot, tempers flare to disrupt our peace. Evil sneaks into our world, bringing with it turmoil and conflict to damage our fellowship.

Like David, we must take an active role in doing what is good and seeking peace. Treat others with kindness, compassion, and brotherly love with a humble spirit. Replace conflict with harmony, smoothing ruffled feathers with sympathetic words.

If we apply Jesus Christ's principle of treating each other as we want to be treated, peace will pursue us.

Almighty God, guide us as we seek
and pursue Your peace in our hearts.

Calming Outlook

And let the peace that comes from Christ rule in your hearts. For as members of one body you are called to live in peace. And always be thankful.

COLOSSIANS 3:15 NLT

Paul gives us clear instructions about the character expected of Christians. Since our hearts once carried the malicious, callous wickedness of the idolatrous world, we are now eager to reveal our new Christ-filled hearts.

No longer do we allow bitterness, wrath, and chaos to dominate our lives. Those attitudes have been replaced with kindness, mercy, and restraint. We forgive others as God in Christ has forgiven us. We let God's love shine through us in our words, deeds, and manners. How can we not rejoice in every opportunity to serve our Lord each day as we share such a wonderful bond of unity with each other? Our Christian love has taken root and continues to grow within us.

When we allow the peace that comes from Christ to rule our hearts, then compassion, gentleness, and forgiveness come through us naturally. And we are always thankful for that calming outlook.

Merciful God, we praise You and thank You for the eternal peace of Christ, which rules in every circumstance of our lives.

Never Alone

*Therefore, since we have been declared righteous by
faith, we have peace with God through our Lord Jesus
Christ. We have also obtained access through Him
by faith into this grace in which we stand, and we
rejoice in the hope of the glory of God.*
ROMANS 5:1–2 HCSB

In these verses, the apostle Paul wasn't describing
peace as a cozy feeling, but the result of an eternal
relationship with our heavenly Father. God declared
us righteous when we put our faith in His Son, Jesus
Christ. No longer His enemies, we are now justified
as His loving children. The peace *of* God became our
peace *with* God.

We can confidently face any trial or difficulty in
the assurance that we have direct access to the Lord.
We are not alone. The Holy Spirit takes every step with
us as our Guide, Conscience, and Comforter.

Our loving Father will bring all of His purposes
for us to fruition at His discretion. Since we are part
of this ongoing process of trials and joys, we take
pleasure in the blessing of peace with God.

*Gracious God, let us find comfort in knowing we have
peace with You in every situation we encounter.
We rejoice in the hope of Your glory.*

Promise Keeper

You are my portion, LORD; I have promised to obey
your words. I have sought your face with all my heart;
be gracious to me according to your promise.
PSALM 119:57–58 NIV

The Lord promised to bless those who obeyed Him,
and the psalmist promised to obey God's words. These
two promises honored the Lord.

The only way we can have fellowship with the Lord
is by knowing His Word. We read, study, and memo-
rize Bible verses to give us a greater understanding
of God's message to us. He has promised to tell us
everything we need to know to get through life, and
He uses the Bible to do it. The book of Proverbs covers
almost all the issues we face today.

In my opinion, one of the most important themes
running through the Word is God's promises or covenants. He promised Sarah a son in her old age. She bore
Isaac. He promised that Abraham's seed would bless
the world. Jesus Christ came through his lineage to
bring the greatest blessing of all time to the world—the
gift of eternal life. He used Joshua to lead the Israelites
into the land He promised them.

God keeps every promise He makes.

How blessed are we, Lord God, as we read Your words.
Help us follow the psalmist's desire to obey them.

A New Tapestry

And we know that God causes everything to work
together for the good of those who love God and
are called according to his purpose for them.
ROMANS 8:28 NLT

God made this promise to those of us who love Him.
He will help us sort out all the details of our lives. He
will use every thread of our tragedies and conflicts,
as well as our joys and blessings, to weave a beautiful
tapestry. The strands of varied colors intertwine to
form a picture of God's purpose. He embroiders in the
dark ones for shading, the bright ones for radiance,
and the midtones for contrast.

The ups and downs of each experience create
a new pattern for a new tapestry. We will adorn our
mansions in heaven with beautiful wall hangings created by God. We won't see the dark threads as our
heartaches but as essential portions that add depth
to the finished image.

As we wind our way through all our circumstances—
the good, the bad, and the mundane—we have the hope
of God's promise to work everything out for His glory.

God, our loving Father, we relinquish our impossible
moments to You to weave them in with Your blessings
for us. We treasure Your glorious handiwork.

At His Appointed Time

The Lord is not slow about His promise, as some count
slowness, but is patient toward you, not wishing for
any to perish but for all to come to repentance.
2 PETER 3:9 NASB

Jesus said to watch for signs of the end of the age and of His return. There would be wars and rumors of wars. Check that off the list. We watch the world news and nod in affirmation. Famines and earthquakes? Check. The torturing and killing of Christians for their faithfulness? Check. Cults leading many astray? Check.

To unbelievers, it appears the world is falling apart. But to us, it means everything is falling into place. At one minute before midnight, our "world" clock has stopped. We're ready to meet Jesus in the clouds, but He hasn't come.

God is never late but always patient. While we wait for Him, He waits for more people to repent. He doesn't want anyone to spend eternity away from His love.

As we grieve for our family and friends who reject Him, He encourages us to continue in our prayers for all to come to salvation through Christ alone.

He will fulfill the promise of His return at His appointed time.

O God in heaven, we pray for our loved ones
who reject Christ. Please soften their
hearts before it's too late.

All Our Days

O God, You have taught me from my youth,
and I still declare Your wondrous deeds. And even
when I am old and gray, O God, do not forsake me,
until I declare Your strength to this generation,
Your power to all who are to come.
PSALM 71:17–18 NASB

This psalmist, presumably King David in his old age, continuously praised the Lord for sustaining him since birth, encouraging him from boyhood, and teaching His truth through adulthood. Even when David's adversaries persistently plotted against him, he continued to hope and praise God for His inexhaustible mercies.

God doesn't throw us away when we become eligible for senior discounts. He doesn't say, "You're done," when we hit a specific birthday. Neither will He abandon us when old age saps our strength. He will continue to use us as long as we have breath. We must teach the generations coming up behind us about God's wondrous deeds and glory.

Just as God continued to deliver David from many troubles and distresses, He will continue to watch over us, even when we're old and weary.

O Lord God, give us Your wisdom and strength to
reach the next generation in our old age.
Use us as long as we have breath.

Rest in Him

*"Come to Me, all you who labor and are heavy laden,
and I will give you rest. Take My yoke upon you and
learn from Me, for I am gentle and lowly in heart,
and you will find rest for your souls. For My
yoke is easy and My burden is light."*
MATTHEW 11:28–30 NKJV

Jesus extended His offer to everyone to receive salvation, to learn, and to serve with Him. All of our labors won't produce salvation because we can't earn it. It is the free gift of God through Jesus Christ. All we have to do is come to Him, and He will give us rest from our futile striving to get to heaven.

The yoke of learning represents disciplined instruction. Like oxen that are yoked to pull the load together, so are we yoked with Jesus to learn His ways. Unlike the scribes, who burdened the people with legalism, Jesus offered to take those burdens on Himself. This He did on the cross.

To serve with Him under His yoke means we work in unison with Him in all we do. He is beside us when we are weary and when we are at rest. Let us rejoice in that wonderful truth.

*We praise You, Father, for taking our
burdens and giving us rest in Jesus.*

Caring for Others

And let us not be weary in well doing: for in due season we shall reap, if we faint not. As we have therefore opportunity, let us do good unto all men, especially unto them who are of the household of faith.

GALATIANS 6:9–10 KJV

While visiting an elderly woman from our church, I noticed her mowed and edged lawn. The leaves were raked, bagged, and set by the curb. I asked if she had hired a lawn service. She hadn't. One of the women from church came by at noon with a meal, saw the neglected grounds, and spent the rest of the day tending to the yard work.

This same precious "yard angel" brought me chicken soup when I developed acute bronchitis. She and her daughter also drove me to my doctor appointments and to the pharmacy. Her husband and two sons came to my aid when home repair needs arose. This family demonstrates the apostle Paul's directive to not grow weary in doing good, especially to those who share our Christian faith. They might be tired from the physical demands of helping others, but they don't grow weary in spirit.

God in heaven, thank You for the blessings of friends who use every opportunity to care for others in the faith. Help us emulate them as they emulate Christ.

Perfect Savior

*For consider Him who endured such hostility
from sinners against Himself, so that you
won't grow weary and lose heart.*
HEBREWS 12:3 HCSB

We toil day and night on a special project, only to have it dismissed as substandard. We share our heart with a potential mate, but we're rejected for another love relationship. Our aches, pains, and illnesses can overwhelm and depress us. How can we not grow weary?

Jesus spent three years in His ministry teaching about the coming kingdom, healing the sick, and driving out demons. He even restored life to a dead friend. The religious leaders and Roman officials dismissed Him as irrelevant, despite the miracles they watched Him perform. He offered the love of the Father to the people He created. They rejected Him, choosing instead love of tradition and love of self. He endured a trusted friend's betrayal. He endured illegal hearings before the Sanhedrin. Then, under orders of Pontius Pilate, He was beaten, flogged, and crucified.

Our afflictions become less wearying when we compare them to what Jesus willingly suffered on our behalf. We love and accept Him for who He is—our perfect Savior.

*Gracious loving Father, thank You for keeping our
perspective in line with Yours.*

Our Refuge

*But striking a place where two seas met, they ran the
ship aground; and the prow stuck fast and remained
immovable, but the stern was being broken
up by the violence of the waves.*

ACTS 27:41 NKJV

Paul warned the centurion guard and the sailors on the
ship that they would sustain heavy damage and loss if
they continued on the journey to Italy. They dismissed
his suggestion. After all, they were qualified seamen
and knew how to handle a ship in a storm. The ship
wrecked on the island of Malta.

Our hectic and frustrating "storms" resemble
being tossed about in a ship without a rudder. We
reject wise counsel because we think we know how to
handle our matters. Or we wait until we've run aground
to ask for help. Then we try gathering the pieces to
rebuild what the tempest destroyed.

Most of our wearying circumstances begin with
small warnings. Storm clouds gather on our horizon
as evidence of developing trouble. Then a rumble of
thunder alerts us of intensifying danger. If we are aware
of the signs, then we can avert the storm's damage
by taking refuge in God's protection. That is the best
time to pray—before we run aground.

*Lord God, thank You for Your protection and
guidance when our circumstances become
tempests to wear us down.*

Help in Our Stumbles

*For what I am doing, I do not understand; for I am
not practicing what I would like to do, but I
am doing the very thing I hate.*

ROMANS 7:15 NASB

A matron in our church frequently hosted a luncheon at her home for the preacher. She invited other congregation members to join them. During the drive to her home, I rehearsed my polite response to the offer of dessert: "No, thank you." I wanted my waistline to shrink, not grow.

As we finished eating, a helper picked up our plates and offered cake and ice cream. I opened my mouth to say, "No, thank you," but out came, "Chocolate cake and vanilla ice cream, please." My mouth betrayed me! Temptation caught me in a weak moment.

Not all of our failings are this amusing. A sip of wine can throw a recovering alcoholic into a binge. A lottery ticket costs only a dollar, except for the addicted gambler who uses the mortgage money to increase the odds of winning.

Even though the Holy Spirit indwells us, we still wearily struggle with our former sinful nature. And so did Christ's apostle Paul. He overcame, and so can we.

*Dear God, when we stumble, You are there to help us
up. Thank You for being willing to strengthen
our resolve, if only we would ask.*

Joy in Distress

You have seen me tossing and turning through the night. You have collected all my tears and preserved them in your bottle! You have recorded every one in your book.
PSALM 56:8 TLB

What a tender image of God's sympathetic love for us—catching our tears in a bottle and recording our heartaches in His book. His loving-kindness is bountiful. Some of us might envision our bottle of tears as a carafe the size of a city's water tank. It could be, for nothing is too large for our heavenly Father.

God gives His loving attention to every aspect of our suffering, from a single tear to our most devastating heartache. He takes into account every offense, every betrayal, and every loss we endure. He knows our pain. He knows the worries that keep us awake at night. And He holds us in His loving arms.

In David's lament psalm, he pleaded for God's help, acknowledged His continuing presence in his life, and offered praise. Following David's example, we can find joy in our distress through God's kindhearted love. He's got our backs—and our tears.

Father God, calm our tossing and turning. Give us Your comfort in our weeping. We place our broken hearts into Your tender embrace.

Because of Who He Is

But God proves His own love for us in that while we were still sinners, Christ died for us!

ROMANS 5:8 HCSB

Jesus told us to love our enemies and pray for those who persecute us. He provided the definitive illustration of this when He died for us—His enemies—and prayed from the cross for those who crucified Him. We cannot fathom a love so deep.

God created us to have fellowship with Him. Adam's sin broke that alliance. How quickly humankind's heart deteriorated from love for God to enmity. And yet, He still loved us even though we remained hostile toward Him. The only way we could be reconciled with the Creator was through the death of His Son, the perfect sacrifice. We cannot fathom a love so enduring.

God loves us not because of who we are but because of who He is. We were helpless, ungodly beings who did nothing to deserve His love. And yet, He poured out His love within our hearts through the Holy Spirit, which bonded us to Him when we believed in Christ as our Savior. We cannot fathom a love so powerful.

Almighty God, we cannot fathom the depth, endurance, or power of Your love for us. We can only thank You by sharing it with others.

Part of Him

For I am convinced that neither death, nor life,
nor angels, nor principalities, nor things present,
nor things to come, nor powers, nor height, nor depth,
nor any other created thing, will be able to separate us
from the love of God, which is in Christ Jesus our Lord.
ROMANS 8:38–39 NASB

God is in control of everything in the universe. There isn't anything or any person, even ourselves, that can separate us from His eternal love.

Death ushers us into His presence to spend eternity with Him. Our Father shares all of life's events with us, wrapping us in His love, whether in sorrow or joy. Satan's demons will fail because we are joined to God through the Holy Spirit. Government rulers forbid owning a Bible, but Christians have hidden His Word in their hearts. There is nothing we can do today or in the future that will cause God to dissolve His fellowship with us. Our courts will rule against preaching His Word, but we can host home Bible studies. The height and depth of His love is beyond measure.

Only God can separate us from His love, but He won't. We are part of Him now—forever!

Loving God, what joy Your inseparable love brings
to us! We praise You and give thanks.

In All Circumstances

He that dwelleth in the secret place of the most High
shall abide under the shadow of the Almighty.
I will say of the LORD, He is my refuge and my
fortress: my God; in him will I trust.

PSALM 91:1–2 KJV

The psalmist used four different names to describe God in these two verses. The most High (*El Elyion*) describes God's strength and sovereignty. Almighty (*El Shaddai*) is drawn from a word that denotes a mountain. He is all-powerful and magnificent like a mountain. LORD (*YHWH*) has a dual meaning: Self-existent One and Redeemer. This name is most commonly related to His holiness, abhorrence of sin, and gracious redemption. God (*Elohim*) means Supreme Deity, the most exalted One who is omniscient and omnipotent.

When we abide with God, He surrounds us on all four sides with His sovereign, magnificent, redeeming, and supreme love. No matter where we go, He provides a refuge for us, His children, under His protective shadow. We can trust the Lord's promise never to leave us or forsake us in any of our circumstances.

Almighty, Most High God, in our distress,
we come to You seeking Your care, security,
protection, and love. You are our refuge and fortress.

Abide in Jesus

"I am the vine, you are the branches. He who abides in Me, and I in him, bears much fruit; for without Me you can do nothing."

JOHN 15:5 NKJV

Eternal life comes through our Vine, the Lord Jesus Christ. Our heavenly Father is the Vinedresser who prunes the healthy branches and cuts away the unproductive ones. God's pruning disciplines and cleanses us so we can produce more fruit. It's better to be pruned than cut from the vine and set aside as dead wood.

Jesus introduced a new commandment, which charges us to love our neighbors as ourselves. This brotherly love bears sweet fruit. Abiding in Christ means obedience to His commandments. If we choose to disobey Jesus, then we will bear sour grapes. Instead of bringing new believers to Him, we would drive them away with a bitter taste in their mouths. We must work together in harmony with Jesus, aiming for the same goal—harvesting crops of ripened, healthy fruit. It's only possible with the Lord.

All of our works reflect back to Christ and our heavenly Father. If we abide in Jesus, then we abide in the Father. And we do not profane God's good name and character.

Thank You, Father, for calling us to be Your branches in Your vineyard and letting us grow in Your Vine, our Savior Jesus Christ.

Powerful Alliance

No one has seen God at any time; if we love one another, God abides in us, and His love is perfected in us. By this we know that we abide in Him and He in us, because He has given us of His Spirit.

1 JOHN 4:12–13 NASB

Because of God's great love for us who profess Christ, He has bound us to Himself through the indwelling of the Holy Spirit. Although we can't see God, we sense His presence within us through our mutual abiding.

The Holy Spirit guides us back to the Lord when we stray. He comforts us in our suffering. He reveals God's wisdom to us when we study His Word. He prays for us when we're deeply grieved or distressed and can't find the words. He helps us with our difficult decisions. He prompts us to forgive those who have hurt us with their words or deeds. He encourages us to love one another as Christ loves us. And He shares our joy when God blesses us in abundance. What a powerful alliance we have in abiding with Him!

We love You, Lord. Let us show others our love for You through the abiding Holy Spirit.

Permanent Relief

For the creation was subjected to futility, not willingly, but because of Him who subjected it in hope; because the creation itself also will be delivered from the bondage of corruption into the glorious liberty of the children of God. For we know that the whole creation groans and labors with birth pangs together until now.

ROMANS 8:20–22 NKJV

The apostle Paul likened God's damaged creation to an expectant mother in labor. In most cases of childbirth, the physical pains begin slowly, with a feeling of pressure. Then they increase in frequency and intensity as the baby is pushed toward the birth canal. Emotions run rampant. Anticipation and fear join with other anxious concerns. Then joy comes when the baby is finally born.

Adam's fall from grace subjected all creation to the penalty of his sin. The whole earth and all it contains are pregnant with the destructive impact of one man's rebellion. As we approach the final days, our trials and tribulations increase. We run the gamut of emotions with each dilemma.

God has planned for the relief of every tribulation. We wait eagerly for His fulfillment of our hope in the resurrection of our bodies.

Then God's joy will replace our tribulations.

Almighty God, as we anticipate the coming relief of every tribulation, we put our trust and hope in You.

Eternal Glory

*For our light affliction, which is but for a moment,
worketh for us a far more exceeding and eternal
weight of glory; while we look not at the things
which are seen, but at the things which are not
seen: for the things which are seen are temporal;
but the things which are not seen are eternal.*

2 Corinthians 4:17–18 kjv

Paul's tribulations in Macedonia were oppressive. They could have caused him to lose heart, but he maintained a hopeful viewpoint. Regardless of his afflictions, he focused on the eternal glory that outweighed any temporary troubles he had to endure this side of heaven.

Paul offers encouragement to us as we suffer various trials and tribulations. The experiences might seem like an eternity. But, compared to the joy that awaits us in the presence of the Lord, the duration is only a moment.

Christ admonished us that in this world we would have tribulation. Paul's troubles began almost immediately after his conversion. Despite that, he kept his focus on the future when he would be resurrected with the risen Lord in his glorified body. We also must embrace that hope as we endure our tribulations.

Eternal Father, as we suffer tribulations in this temporal world, we trust in Your promise of a far more exceeding and eternal weight of glory in eternity.

Let Us Not Lose Heart

Therefore I ask you not to lose heart at my tribulations on your behalf, for they are your glory.
EPHESIANS 3:13 NASB

Paul had suffered to bring the hope of Christ to the people in Ephesus. He had concerns that word of his tribulations might discourage them. He assured them that their faithfulness to the Lord brought him joy. His directive to not lose heart is relevant for us today.

When we endure tribulations on behalf of others because we shared the Gospel, let us not lose heart. Our joy will be made complete as we sow seeds of faith in a hostile world.

We pray for God to end our tribulations or lighten our burdens, but the answers might not come immediately. Let us not lose heart. God is never late. Waiting for His reply strengthens our trust and obedience.

When we suffer for doing good or serving others, let us not lose heart. We are storing up wonderful rewards in heaven.

Let us not lose heart when trials come because of everyday burdens. Our life here is fleeting. Tribulations will not follow us into eternity when the Lord calls us home in His time.

Thank You, Lord, for reminding us not to lose heart during our tribulations. We have Your promise of future joy and comfort.

Follow Jesus

The serpent said to the woman, "You surely will not die! For God knows that in the day you eat from it your eyes will be opened, and you will be like God, knowing good and evil."

GENESIS 3:4–5 NASB

Eve became the first casualty of the war between good and evil when she questioned God's sovereignty after hearing Satan's deceptive words. Temptation entered first through the lust of her eyes as she saw that the tree was good for food. Then came the lust of her flesh as she tasted the first delicious bite. From that downward spiral, she added the pride of life in sharing the new discovery with her husband. "Look what I found, Adam!"

Because Adam and Eve sinned, all their children, grandchildren, great-grandchildren—and all of us and beyond—would be born sinners. Without Christ, we're all under the death penalty because of their rebellion.

The battle continues within us. Satan ignores us until we choose to follow Jesus. Then he strikes hard to keep us in his wicked camp. When all his efforts fail, he tries his "Eve tactics" to neutralize us. We are useful to him if we are useless to the Lord.

Dear God, let our eyes look only to You, our taste hunger only for Your Word, and our pride be humbled in serving only You.

Supreme Indeed

"But stretch out Your hand and strike everything he owns, and he will surely curse You to Your face."
JOB 1:11 HCSB

In Job's spiritual battle, Satan suggested to God that the man served Him only for selfish gain and not in faithful love. The motive for the devil's challenge was not so much to test Job's loyalty, but more to discredit God's supremacy. Would He continue to guard Job or take down the hedge of protection?

Job maintained that all the calamities were not because of his sin. Despite statements to the contrary, he knew in his heart that he was true to his faith. And so did God.

In Job's steadfast love and loyalty, he proved God's almighty supremacy. And God proved that Job was a man of unwavering integrity. Satan lost the challenge. God restored all that Job had lost, and then some.

When our trials come at us in tidal waves as Job's did, do we check our loyalty levels to the Lord? In our prayers for relief and deliverance, let us praise God for His power and authority in His love for us. We can prove to the adversary that our God is supreme indeed.

We praise You, Lord. Even when we can't comprehend Your plans for us, we know You stand with us in our battles.

Word of God

*Then Jesus was led by the Spirit into the
wilderness to be tempted by the devil.*

MATTHEW 4:1 NIV

Jesus had to face His opponent. After Jesus' baptism
and anointing, the Holy Spirit led Him to the place
God had planned for this confrontation.

Satan appeared in the wilderness, ready for battle with his three snares of temptation. If he could
catch Jesus with one trap, it would foil God's plan for
humankind's redemption. One slipup would disqualify
the Savior.

After a forty-day fast, Jesus was hungry. Yet He
would not use His power to manipulate matter to satisfy His personal needs. He refused to throw Himself
into danger to test God's protection. Satan offered
Him a quick way to the kingdom that didn't include
His death. But Jesus knew His death and resurrection
were the keys to salvation.

Jesus thwarted each of Satan's snares with the
sword of the Spirit—the Word of God.

Satan waits for us in our wilderness experiences
with his tempting snares. We have the same sword that
Jesus used. The Word of God will prepare us for our
spiritual battles. We must read the Bible on a regular
basis, study it, and learn it to be able to utilize it.

*Heavenly Father, train us to use our weapon—
Your Word—effectively when Satan tempts
us in our spiritual battles.*

Proof of Victory

"Nevertheless do not rejoice in this, that the spirits are subject to you, but rather rejoice because your names are written in heaven."

LUKE 10:20 NKJV

Jesus chose seventy disciples to go ahead of Him to every city or place He intended to visit. He sent them out, not en masse but in pairs. Although they could cover more ground, this made them vulnerable as lambs in the midst of wolves. They had to rely on God's protection.

Jesus gave them authority to heal the sick, crush the evil spirits, and subdue the power of the enemy, Satan. The success of these seventy over demons proved Satan's power was beaten. Jesus said to them, "I saw Satan fall like lightning from heaven" (Luke 10:18 NKJV). They had reason to celebrate this victory, but the greater joy was that their names were recorded in heaven.

We face spiritual battles all day, every day as we serve on the mission field in our specific calling. Preaching from a downtown corner, leading a children's Sunday school class, writing books and articles, to name a few, spread God's Word. He records our names in heaven as we work for Him. This is proof of our victory.

Lord of heaven and earth, we rejoice in knowing our names are recorded as Your servants. We are encouraged to continue our fight in the battle.

Ready for Battle

Therefore, take up the full armor of God,
so that you will be able to resist in the evil day,
and having done everything, to stand firm.

EPHESIANS 6:13 NASB

We are in spiritual warfare with a formidable, strategic, and methodical adversary—the demonic soldiers of Satan. They are structured in their ranks and prepared for combat.

To uphold and safeguard our specific missions for the Lord, God has equipped us with protective and defensive gear. Sitting on the shelf, next to our dusty Bible, this armor is impressive but useless. It protects us only when we wear it.

Therefore, God orders us to put on the belt of truth, which holds our integrity in place. Then we don the breastplate of righteousness to protect our hearts from Satan's attacks. We shod our feet for our walk to spread the Gospel of peace. Next we hold up the shield of our faith to extinguish Satan's dispiriting arrows. The helmet of salvation keeps our thoughts pure and aligned with God's message. The sword of the Spirit, God's holy Word, is the only weapon we need. We cover the whole armor with prayer to God. Now, strengthened in His courage, we are ready for battle.

Holy God, we praise You for You have armed
us with courage and the assurance of
victory against a powerful foe.

Supreme Commander

Take your share of suffering as a good soldier of Jesus Christ, just as I do; and as Christ's soldier, do not let yourself become tied up in worldly affairs, for then you cannot satisfy the one who has enlisted you in his army.

2 TIMOTHY 2:3–4 TLB

All of the armed forces require discipline and solidarity in their military servicemen. If soldiers allow personal affairs and conflicts to distract them, they put all others in the group at risk. Focus and obedience are important factors in keeping the enemy at bay.

As Christians, we are soldiers for Christ. We enlisted when we first believed in Him as our Savior. The evil one drew a target on us in that moment. This foe hungers for wrath and hatred.

In our camaraderie with other Christian soldiers, we endure the struggles of our spiritual battles together. Providing our best service to the Lord must be our priority. We can't allow worldly clutter to blind us to our true calling. This will entail suffering hardships as we endure ridicule, or worse, for our faithfulness. But this is required to satisfy and please our Supreme Commander.

God, our Father, we are Your soldiers, willing to fight the good fight until You have secured our victory.

Extraordinary Input

For we wanted to come to you—I, Paul, more than once—and yet Satan hindered us.

1 THESSALONIANS 2:18 NASB

Paul tried to find a way to return to Thessalonica, but doing so would harm his friend Jason. The synagogue leaders had forced Paul to leave the city and held Jason responsible for keeping the preacher from coming back. He would forfeit his pledge or bond if they caught Paul there again.

We don't see Satan visibly working in this account of Paul's harassment, but he most assuredly was in the middle of it. The devil uses anything and anyone he can to prevent us from spreading the truth of Jesus Christ. Think of how many times we, like Paul, made arrangements to meet with lost souls to tell them about Jesus Christ. Then bizarre events or circumstances arose to block that get-together. But the Lord provided an alternate way to reach them. When Satan hinders our plan A, God has a plan B.

Since Paul was forbidden to return, he sent Timothy to Thessalonica to help the new believers grow in their faith. Timothy's visit was God's plan B.

Watch for the Lord's extraordinary input during our battles. He will always amaze us.

All-powerful God, thank You for intervening at the right moment with Your encouraging plan B.

God's Timing

And whenever those possessed by evil spirits caught sight of him, the spirits would throw them to the ground in front of him shrieking, "You are the Son of God!" But Jesus sternly commanded the spirits not to reveal who he was.

MARK 3:11–12 NLT

God ordered the timing of Christ's ministry, suffering, crucifixion, resurrection, and ascension down to the second. Each step of the process had to be followed precisely in God's time for His purpose.

Satan's demons tried to upset the sequence with their premature proclamation that Jesus was the Christ. If they could rile the chief priests, scribes, and elders ahead of schedule, then Jesus wouldn't be able to call the twelve apostles into service. The sick would not be healed. The demon-possessed would not be cleansed. Lazarus would remain dead in his tomb. The Roman soldiers would crucify an unknown rebel.

Jesus knew God's timing had been set. He commanded the evil spirits not to tell who He was. Inasmuch as they took their orders from the devil, they were only angels. Jesus was God in the flesh. His orders overruled Satan's.

God's timing is absolute in our spiritual battles too. He has set the sequential steps in our circumstances to fulfill His purposes.

Holy Father, grant us the wisdom to yield to Your power, control, and timing.

175

God Wins

The devil, who deceived them, was cast into the lake
of fire and brimstone where the beast and the false
prophet are. And they will be tormented
day and night forever and ever.
REVELATION 20:10 NKJV

Spiritual warfare in heaven began long before the creation of the universe and all its components. Satan rebelled and deceived a third of God's angels to follow him. He deluded himself in believing he is as powerful as his Creator. But he is merely an angel. Powerful, yes, but his power is limited to what God allows. He is clever but doesn't possess God's wisdom. He is still a created being with a beginning and an ending. And he knows this.

Satan has been biting and chomping at us since the fall in Eden. God promised to redeem His humans but offered no salvation for the fallen angels. Their destination remained unchangeable. While we spend our eternal life in the awesomeness of God's glory, they will spend eternal death in deserved torment. Satan will lose the war.

When our struggles overwhelm us and the world seems upside down, let us take courage in the truth of God's Word that in the end of this time, God wins!

Glorious heavenly Father, You have given us
hope with the good news that, in the end,
we will share the victory with You.

Birthright

The Spirit Himself testifies with our spirit that we are children of God, and if children, heirs also, heirs of God and fellow heirs with Christ, if indeed we suffer with Him so that we may also be glorified with Him.
ROMANS 8:16–17 NASB

My siblings and I recently had to prove our birthright for an inheritance from our dad. The challenging party asked for testimony from a nonfamily witness to Dad's transaction. That business deal occurred sixty years ago. Anyone who observed it had gone to his or her reward.

What greater witness do we have to attest to our heavenly inheritance than God Himself? The Holy Spirit indwells us at the moment of salvation, and then He claims us as His children. When we suffer, He suffers with us. When we rejoice, He rejoices with us. Being born again into the family of God, we have the assurance that we will never endure hardships alone. As fellow heirs with Christ, we will also share in His glory. We will take part in the rich blessings of His kingdom.

This gives us hope for the near future—as God nurtures us in this mortal life—and the eternal future—where we will be with Him forever.

Gracious and loving Father, thank You for the blessing of being Your heirs through our Savior, Jesus Christ.

Blessed

Blessed is the nation whose God is the LORD; and the people whom he hath chosen for his own inheritance.
PSALM 33:12 KJV

The United States of America was established on Judeo-Christian principles. The founding fathers used scriptures from Deuteronomy to create our Constitution. They looked to the Lord for guidance. In His righteousness, God led them. Because we proclaimed the Lord as our King from the beginning, He blessed this nation abundantly.

This psalm was written about the nation of Israel, God's chosen inheritance. But we who have been grafted into His family tree can also affirm His blessings. But only if we maintain our belief that God is the Lord. We have a silent majority of Christians in our country. Some are suffering under persecution for their steadfast belief in Christ. Others are ridiculed because they study the Bible. Elected officials scoff at God's Word.

It is possible, with God's help, for us to turn our country back to Him. Through our continuous prayer, diligent preaching of God's Word, and endurance through persecution, others will choose to follow Christ. Then let us declare to the world that our nation is blessed because our God is the Lord.

O Lord, our God, forgive our nation's leaders for turning away from You. Help us be Your light to lead our nation back to Your abundant blessings.

A Crown of Life

*Blessed is the one who perseveres under trial because,
having stood the test, that person will receive
the crown of life that the Lord has
promised to those who love him.*

JAMES 1:12 NIV

The first time we lift weights, our biceps ache. But we continue with the exercise to strengthen those muscles. The stronger our biceps become, the less they ache. We can now lift heavier weights. As we continue with this bodybuilding course, we enjoy the blessings of a healthy and toned physique.

A similar strengthening is true in our trials or hardships. As we persevere for Christ, withstanding the painful soreness, we build strength of character. The effectiveness of our faith grows and matures in our tests of endurance. Instead of praying for God to lessen our burdens, let us pray for Him to give us stronger backs.

Peter wrote that if we are reviled for the name of Christ, we are blessed with the Spirit of glory. Those who berate us for our good deeds will be put to shame.

The promise of our crown will be fulfilled in our eternal life as we accept God's rewards for our stead-fast service.

*Father in heaven, bless us as we persevere
under trial. Give us the strength to carry
these burdens in Christ's name.*

More Blessings

Bless the Lord, O my soul, and all that is within me,
bless His holy name. Bless the Lord, O my soul,
and forget none of His benefits.
PSALM 103:1–2 NASB

Our heavenly Father forgives our sins. He heals our sicknesses and makes His presence known during spiritual attacks. He delivers us from the pits of despair and covers us with His mercy and compassion. We can't measure His everlasting love for us, His children.

Do we look for God's many blessings when we suffer? I recall how He numbed my pain when my husband passed into eternity. As I looked at the lifeless body in the hospital bed, I saw an empty tomb. I knew his soul was with Christ.

When a former employer assailed me with slanderous lies, the Lord pulled me out of that cesspool of innuendoes and harassment. He affirmed that His greater purpose for me was to write about His love.

When a longtime friend betrayed my trust, God showed me, through His Word, the preciousness of true, Christian fellowship.

As we praise the Lord in our difficult situations, He pours out more blessings on us.

Let us continually give thanks to Him, even when we suffer.

Holy Lord, we come to You in reverential awe,
giving thanks for Your countless blessings.

Only with God

We will sing for joy over your victory, and in the
name of our God we will set up our banners.
May the LORD fulfill all your petitions.

PSALM 20:5 NASB

We pray to the Lord for His victory in our conflicts.
Since we are joined to Him through the Holy Spirit,
our battles are His and so are our victories.

The Lord answers our prayers in our days of trouble. We trust in Him to be our sanctuary. He remembers our faithfulness and forgets our transgressions.
Everything we have is from His bounty.

While our enemies take pride in their perceived
domination, we boast in the Lord. He is mightier than
they. We might doubt His power when earnest prayers
fail to vanquish obstacles that prevent us from reaching our goals. That is a normal human reaction. But,
as with Paul's thorn, those obstacles serve a purpose.
When we've done all we can to no avail, we must trust
God completely. His Word assures us that He will
fulfill all our petitions by His methods and in His time.

Our victories over difficulties are possible only
with God.

O Lord our God, we praise You for our hard-
won triumphs over our enemy—for the triumphs
You've won for us in the past and those to come.

Mustard Seed Faith

And without faith it is impossible to please God,
because anyone who comes to him must believe
that he exists and that he rewards those
who earnestly seek him.

Hebrews 11:6 niv

All the men and women listed in Hebrews 11 believed in only one Deity, our Creator, God the Father. Their faith in God's promise of future blessings gave them hope.

Noah pleased the Lord because he trusted His word. He had never seen a flood, yet he built the ark and rounded up the animals. Abraham passed God's test by offering up Isaac. His promised son with Sarah was the only route to the Messiah. Abraham believed so profoundly that God would fulfill His promise, he didn't hesitate to obey. Rahab risked her life to save Joshua's spies. She claimed, "For the Lord your God, he is God in the heavens above and on the earth beneath" (Joshua 2:11 esv).

If we consider this great cloud of witnesses and their depth of faith, we might feel insignificant. But these were ordinary people like you and me.

Jesus said nothing would be impossible to us if we have faith the size of a mustard seed. Even this faith pleases God. As mustard seeds grow into huge trees, so our faith will mature.

Our God in heaven, we put our faith and trust in You.

All Things

I can do all things through Christ who strengthens me.
PHILIPPIANS 4:13 NKJV

The late Hudson Taylor, missionary to China, wisely said, "I have found that there are three stages in every great work of God; first, it is impossible, then it is difficult, then it is done."

When the Israelites were caught between Pharaoh's army and the Red Sea, they viewed their situation as impossible. Did they consider the difficult task of building boats to carry them across the body of water? God parted the sea for them, and it was done.

David often found himself caught in impossible circumstances, but, in answer to his prayers, the Lord rescued him. The apostles suffered dreadful persecutions and assaults, but they remained faithful as the Lord strengthened them and delivered them.

As Paul rejoiced in the Lord for the church in Philippi, he assured them that God would be with them as He was with Paul.

Regardless of our circumstances—which might seem impossible, then difficult—God is here to guide and care for us. We can do all things through Christ who gives us strength, and God's great works will be done.

Gracious heavenly Father, thank You for Your promise that nothing is impossible for You.

Acknowledgments

I am truly grateful to all my loved ones for their prayers and support while I toiled to write this devotional. I especially want to acknowledge local Christian authors Sharron Cosby, Donna Mumma, and Jan Powell, who took time from their busy schedules to assist me with critiques, edits, and polishing. And to Faith Nordine for her eagle-eyed oversight of the finished work. Their expertise helped me produce this good fruit for the Lord. I praise God for providing this wonderful opportunity for me to share His love.

Scripture Index

Janet Ramsdell Rockey is a freelance Christian author in Tampa, Florida. Her many contributions to other Barbour publications include the devotionals *Discovering God in Everyday Moments* and *Fear Less, Pray More.*

Discover a Deeper Prayer Life with. . .

The Prayer Map for Women

This purposeful prayer journal is a fun and creative way to more fully experience the power of prayer. Each page guides you to write out thoughts, ideas, and lists. . .creating a specific "map" for you to follow as you talk to God. Each map includes a spot to record the date, so you can look back on your prayers and see how God has worked in your life. *The Prayer Map for Women* will not only encourage you to spend time talking with God about the things that matter most. . .it will also help you build a healthy spiritual habit of continual prayer for life!

Spiral Bound / 978-1-68322-557-7 / $7.99